D1633543

© PETER WEBB

Rolling Stones In Their Own Words

Compiled by David Dalton
and Mick Farren

Exclusive distributors
Book Sales Limited, 78 Newman Street, London
London W1P 3LA.
Quick Fox, 33 West 60th Street, New York,
N.Y.10023, USA.
Book Sales Pty. Limited, 27 Clarendon Street,
Artarmon, 2064, Australia.

Omnibus Press
London/New York/Sydney/Tokyo/Cologne

Designed by Chris Harris
Cover design by Pearce Marchbank and Perry Neville
Cover tinting by Ken Slater
Picture research by Jane Coke
Series design by Pearce Marchbank

We would like to thank Coco Pekelis whose help was
invaluable in sifting through hundreds of rock
magazines, music trade papers and taped interviews
and extracting the pithiest kernels of the World's
Wordiest Rock'n'Roll Group. In collecting the raw
material for this book we are indebted to Mr. Tom
Beach who generously contributed items from his
great library of Rolling Stones' papers, periodicals
and printed matter.
Our thanks also to Jennifer Rudderham
and our apologies to anyone not credited
who should have been.

Introduction ©Copyright 1980 David Dalton
This book ©Copyright 1980 Omnibus Press
(a division of Book Sales Limited).

All rights reserved. No part of this book may be
reproduced in any form or by any electronic or
mechanical means, including information, storage
and retrieval systems, without permission in writing
from the publisher, except by a reviewer who may
quote brief passages in a review.

ISBN 0 86001 541 6
UK order No. OP 4040 1

Typeset by Letterbox Limited, Rivington Street,
London.
Printed in England by Camelot Press Limited,
Southampton.

CHRISTOPHER SYKES

Introduction.

"I thought we stood for infinity."
Mick Jagger, late Twentieth Century.

Sophisticated, wordly-wise and consummate performers the Stones have always been too aware of their rôle as entertainers to fall into the lethal fallacy of living out their vinyl fantasies on the street.

However, like most musicians, the Stones in print tend to speak in much the same way as they make their music. Between the lines in this book, for instance, you can hear Mick's arch, shifting, multiphrenic voice which has made him such a master of mimicry and mime as a singer, Keith's wry and spare delivery and his cool eye casting about equally on the darkness and the light, Charlie's solid solipsisms and good-natured pleasantries, Bill's basic, grounded insights (his description of how the band works together in the *Performance* chapter alone is worth anything so far written about the Stones), Brian's prolix proclamations, Mick Taylor's subtle asides, ("I have the rare distinction of being the only person so far to have left the Stones and *lived*."), and Ron Wood's straightforward goodtime raps.

We have attempted to give every member of the Stones an equal voice, but Jagger, inevitably, does most of the talking here. Nik Cohn once said of Mick that he "early on devoted himself to a life of masks... there is nothing about him that you could swear was absolutely genuine, no absolute core." Far from being a telling criticism, this is a tribute to Mick's integrity and his art.

These selected sayings of the Stones should really come with stage directions. We've left them in where they were there in the original. Where there aren't any you're welcome to supply them.

While reading these quotations bear in mind that any encounter with the unflappable Mick with his cat-like agility for slipping out of tight corners is as likely to be a performance or a verbal fencing match as it is the proverbial interview. The context is often as important as the content with the Stones' music as it is with their words. Whereas much of Dylan's raps can stand quite absurdly on their own surrealistic hind legs, the Stones are never deadpan, always relative and subject only to the laws of the well-known 'Ruby Tuesday Effect'. You just can't hang a name on them, especially when they change their minds – if not every new day – at least as often as they change their strings.

Finally, remember that the quotations in this book cover a relatively recent time scale; most were drawn from interviews and articles about the Stones that have appeared since 1967. The reason for this is that until the appearance of "serious" rock journals like *Crawdaddy* and *Rolling Stone* few journalists bothered to interview the Stones or even knew what to ask them anyway.

First came the working press, a cynical lot at best, and they were only ever interested in exploiting the more ludicrous and unsavoury aspects of the band (viz.: "Air Pollution: The Rock Band That Hasn't Taken A Bath In A Year" or "Drugs, Nude Girl In Fur Rug Found In Raid On Stones Party"). The fan magazines were hardly more illuminating (*Rave* girl Dawn James pays a surprise visit to Mick's flat and the result is an Out-Of-This-World exclusive!!! We find out Mick's Secret Fear and Reveal All!!!) These 'fax' usually turned out to be that Mick likes tall girls, driving alone at night, yellow socks, money and thick steaks well-done. The underground press saw them as psychotrophic emblems and catalysts for the almost always imminent "violent revolution" ("Lookatus! Brainbell Jongleur And The Four Hip Malchicks"). And in the Seventies the press came full circle as the Stones entered the jet-set gossip mills with old war horses like Liz, Jackie O and Margaret Trudeau ("Stones Abduct Premier's Wife Following Heroin Bust"). Well, as Chuck Berry said recently: "Plus ça change..." And now, we'll just leave it up to the boys in the band to tell their own tale in their own inimitable style.
David Dalton.

Prelude.

FLORIDA, 1975/ANNIE LIEBOWITZ (COLORIFIC)

I can remember Mick practising with a group of boys outside our house in Beckwith. They called themselves Little Boy Blue and the Blues Boys. We used to sit in the next room and crease up with laughter. It was lovely but so loud! I always heard more of Mick than I saw of him. I didn't dream they were serious. I thought it was all just for fun.
Mrs. Taylor, (neighbour of the Jaggers and mother of original group member Dick Taylor).

I would have preferred him to become a sportsman, but Mick set off right from the start to be independent. He was about thirteen or fourteen when we found he was listening to pop music. Eventually he and his friends graduated to the bottom of the garden. While one of them played, Mick and the others would sing. His mother and I never interfered because it used to sound quite good . . . He worked hard for his O-levels, although he was always a rebel at school. In the holidays after he took A-levels he had an ice-cream tricycle to earn pocket money. I remember taking the exam results to him and he couldn't believe how good they were. In 1960 Alexis Korner asked Mick to sing at the Marquee. He phoned my wife several times to say we should go along and see him, but we never got round to it. Then Mick joined another group, and I went along to buy the instruments – or at least stand in the background with the money. I didn't realise how well he was getting on till he started using the phone a great deal. It was only when they grew their hair long that a change came about. At first he and his group were just the sort of youngsters any parent could be proud of.
Joe Jagger, (Mick's father).

You couldn't help being aware of Mick because he seemed alive where the other kids would just sink down in their chairs. He questioned authority – he'd ask why, which was unusual then.
Ian Harris (Mick's form master at Dartford Grammar School).

In The Beginning.

My mum is very working class, my father bourgeois, because he had a reasonably good education, so I came from somewhere in between that. Neither one nor the other. *Mick Jagger.*

I used to pose in front of the mirror at home, I was hopeful. The only thing I was lacking was a bit of bread to buy an instrument. But I got the moves off first, and I got the guitar later. *Keith Richards.*

When I was very, very young I used to listen to everything from the BBC to Radio Luxembourg. If a child is musical, you can see that in children of two years old, especially nowadays. You'll see some children of two years old dance and others that don't, which doesn't mean to say that they'll become musicians – just that they're aware of music and, by the time they're around three, they'll distinguish between the kind of music they like and the kind they don't.

You see, we didn't have a record player at home and my immediate family wasn't really musical, and Chris was only about two at the time and as far as I was concerned he was nothing more than a punch bag and I used to beat him up regularly, but then that's quite a common thing with brothers.

It wasn't until I was about twelve that I became really interested in pop. *Mick Jagger.*

Brian was from Cheltenham, a very genteel town full of old ladies, where it used to be fashionable to go and take the baths once a year at Cheltenham Spa. The water is very good because it comes out of the hills, it's spring water. It's a Regency thing, you know, Beau Brummel, around that time. Turn of the 19th century. Now it's a seedy sort of place full of aspirations to be an aristocratic town. It rubs off on anyone who comes from there. *Keith Richards.*

When I was thirteen the first person I really admired was Little Richard. I wasn't particularly fond of Elvis or Bill Haley . . . they were very good, but for some reason they didn't appeal to me. I was more into Jerry Lee Lewis, Chuck Berry and a bit later Buddy Holly.

There was a lot of TV then, *Cool For Cats, 6.5 Special* and *Oh Boy,* and I saw a lot of people on those shows. But rock started over here around 1955, which was a bit before all that. I mean, I missed all that teddy boy era, I wasn't into that at all. I never even saw it, except for the tail end, and I wasn't particularly impressed. *Mick Jagger.*

I really, literally, got myself thrown out of school. I was living at home but I had to go every day. When you think that kids, all they really want to do is learn, watch how it's done and try to figure out why and leave it at that. You're going to school to do something you want to do and they manage to turn the whole thing around and make you hate them.
Keith Richards.

When I was around thirteen or fourteen, I became interested in blues firstly when I found out that it as much as existed. It was never played on the radio and, if it was, it was only by accident. Things that were hits in America, but never over here. *Mick Jagger.*

American R&B stars in Britain? No, they don't make it big over in Britain. I reckon there are three reasons why they don't click with the British teenager fans. One, they're old; two, they're black; three, they're ugly. This image bit is very important – though I must say it doesn't

KEITH RICHARDS

had come from. Broonzy first. He and Josh White were considered to be the only living black bluesmen still playing. So let's get that together, I thought, that can't be right. Then I started to discover Robert Johnson and those cats. You could never get their records though. One heard about them. On one hand I was playing all that folk stuff on the guitar. The other half of me was listenin' to all that rock 'n' roll. Chuck Berry, and sayin' yeah, yeah. *Keith Richards,* 1971.

Mick Meets Keith.

Someone once compared you and Keith to Romulus and Remus – both suckled from a she-wolf's tit.

[Laughing] We're very close, and always have been. He was born my brother by accident by different parents. . . That sounds all right to me. . . *Mick Jagger,* 1978.

When did your friendship with Keith Richards begin?

Well, we went to school together when we were about seven.

Were you aware of his presence?

Yeah, we lived in the same block. We weren't great friends, but we knew each other. We also knew each other when we left school. . . I went to Grammar School while Keith went to another school in the same village, so I used to see Keith riding to school on his bike. Then I saw him again when he used to catch the train to get to

matter to us. But the Americans have helped get things going in Britain . . . their influence is big if their popularity isn't. *Keith Richards,* 1966.

I subsequently became aware that Big Bill Broonzy was a blues singer and Muddy Waters was also a blues singer and they were all really the same and it didn't matter. There were no divisions and I'd realised that by the time I was fifteen. *Mick Jagger.*

So you go there and you get your packet of five Weights [cigarettes] a day. Everybody's broke. . . and the best thing that's going on is in the bog [toilet] with the guitars. There's always some cat sneaked out going through his latest Woody Guthrie tune or Jack Elliot. Everybody's into that kind of music as well. So when I went to art school I was thrown into that end of it too. Before that I was just into Little Richard. I was rockin' away, avoidin' the bicycle chains and the razors in those dance halls. The English get crazy. They're calm, but they were really violent then, those cats. Those suits cost them $150, which is a lot of money. Jackets down to here. Waist-coats. Leopardskin lapels. . . amazing. It was really "Don't step on mah blue suede shoes." It was down to that.

But then I started to get into where it

MICK JAGGER

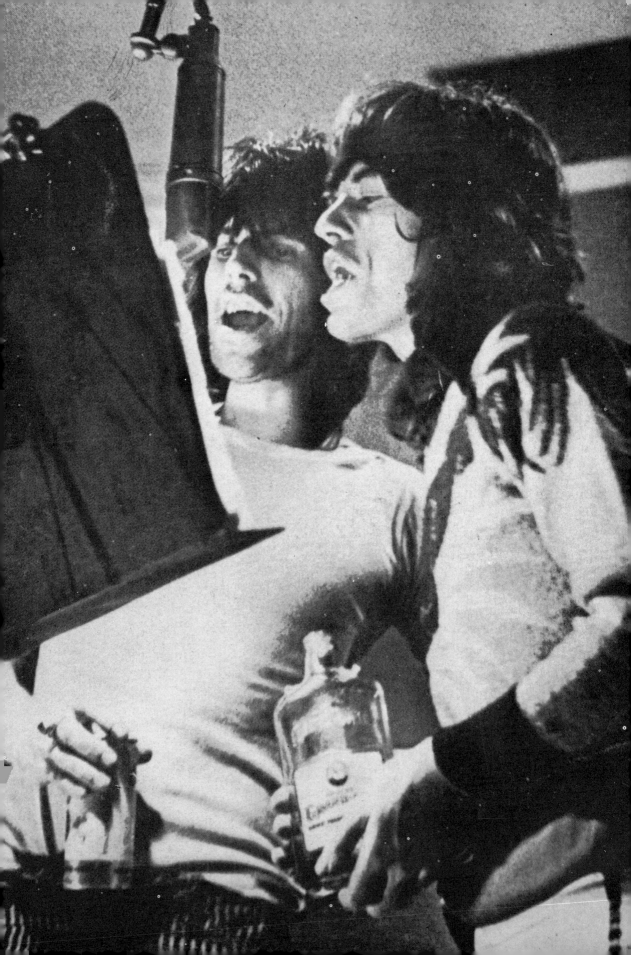

THE DARTFORD DELTA

school and I was on the same train to attend college.

When did you decide that you wanted to play music together?

I don't really know when it was. . . Off-hand. I think it was when we were around seventeen. I used to go round to his house and play records and guitar, then after that we'd go to other people's houses. We just used to play anything. . . Chuck Berry stuff.

Had you started to play guitar by then?

Yeah. I had started about then.

There was traditional jazz and skiffle –

people tend to forget just how enormous that was. I mean, the big thing then was to form a skiffle group, which was a very easy thing to do and was what most bands of the day did. But they were also playing rock 'n' roll numbers.

Nearly every guitarist was a folk-player, but they also played 'Baby Let's Play House' or whatever was on the charts that week. And that was it.

And that's really where English rock 'n' roll started . . . With skiffle groups.
Mick Jagger, 1974.

It's strange 'cause I knew Mick when I was really young . . . five, six, seven. We used to hang out together. Then I moved and

didn't see him for a long time. I once met him selling ice-creams outside the public library. I bought one. He was trying to make extra money.

How things were at the start is something. It's when everybody's got short hair. And everybody thought it was long. I mean, we were really being put down like shit then for having long hair. Really. Now, people go to offices with longer hair.

When I went to art school, people were just starting to grow their hair and loosen up. It's amazing – Lennon, all those people were already playing. I hadn't really thought about playing. I was still just jiving to it. I went straight into this art school, and I heard these cats playing, heard they were laying down some Broonzy songs. And I suddenly realised it goes back a lot further than just the two years I'd been listening. And I picked up the nearest guitar and started learning from these cats. I learned from all these amateur art school people. One cat knew how to play 'Cocaine Blues' very well, another cat knew how to play something else very well. There were a lot better guitar players at school than me.

And one day I met Jagger again, man. Of all places, on the fucking train. I was going to school and he was going up to the London School of Economics. It

WITH IAN STEWART ON MARACAS. 1963/REX FEATURES

was about 1960. I've never been able to get this one together, it's so strange. I had these two things going and not being able to plug them together, playing guitar like all the other cats, folk, a little blues. But you can't get the sounds from the States. Maybe once every six months someone'll come through with an album, an Arhoolie album of Fred McDowell. And you'd say "There's another cat! That's another one". Just blowing my mind, like one album every six months.

So I get on this train one morning and there's Jagger and under his arm he has four or five albums. I haven't seen him since the time I bought an ice-cream off him, and we haven't hung around since we were five, six, ten years. We recognised each other straight off. "Hi, man," I say. "Where ya going?" he say. And under his arm, he's got Chuck Berry and Little Walter, Muddy Waters. "You're into Chuck Berry, man, really?" That's a coincidence. He said, "Yeah, I

got a few more albums. Been writing away to this, uh, Chess Records in Chicago and got a mailing list thing and . . got it together, you know?" So I invited him up to my place for a cup of tea. He started playing me these records and I really turned on to it. We were both still living in Dartford, on the edge of London, and I was still in art school.

There was another cat at art school named Dick Taylor, who later got the Pretty Things together. Mick found out. "Oh, you play?" he said to me. That's what amazed him. Mick had been singing with some rock and roll bands, doing Buddy Holly. Buddy Holly was in England as solid as Elvis. Everything that came out was a record smash number one. By about '58, it was either Elvis or Buddy Holly. It was split into two camps. The Elvis fans were the heavy leather boys and the Buddy Holly ones all somehow looked like Buddy Holly.

Mick was the only one who was still

hovering because he was more heavily committed to the London School of Economics and he was being supported by a government grant, and his parents and all that. So he had a heavier scene to break away from than me because they were very pleased to kick me out anyway. And Brian, too, they were glad to kick out. From university for making some chick pregnant or something.
Keith Richards.

The Flat Off Fulham Road.

It was all pretty much down to Mick, Keith and Brian who were at school together and then sharing the same flat. They were listening to stuff all the time and trying to work out things like those intricate Jimmy Reed guitar runs that interlaced, while Brian was sounding really great on those Elmore James bottleneck runs and those exciting Bo Diddley rhythms. So as you can see it was pretty much in the hands of the three of them. Charlie and I just slotted in.
Bill Wyman.

Brian was the one who kept us all together then. Mick was still going to school. I'd dropped out. So we decided we'd got to live in London to get it together. Time to break loose. So everybody left home, upped and got this pad in London. Chelsea. Just Mick and myself and Brian.

We had the middle floor. The top floor was sort of two school teachers tryin' to keep a straight life. God knows how they managed it. Two guys trainin' to be school teachers, they used to throw these bottle parties. All these weirdos, we used to think they were weirdos, were as straight as. . . havin' their little parties up there, all dancing around to Duke Ellington. Then when they'd zonked out, we'd go up there and nick all the bottles. Get a big bag, Brian and I, get all the beer bottles and the next day, we'd take 'em to the pub to get the money on 'em.
Keith Richards, 1971.

Downstairs was livin' four old whores from Liverpool. Isn't that a coincidence. "Allo dahlin' 'ow are ya? Awright??" Real old boots they were I don't know how they made their bread, working. . . They used to sort of nurse people and keep us together when we really got out of it.
Keith Richards, 1971.

I'd been playing for just about two years and I had a couple of bands in that time, formed from local kids, people I was working with or lived 'round the corner. None of us could play very well. All the local bands were playing Shadows stuff, Ventures stuff, all those semi-instrumental groups, because there were never really any good singers about. So most of the bands had an echo chamber and a good lead guitarist who could play 'FBI' and all that shit, and experiment and try and play some American music, but it was always the wrong stuff – it was 'Poetry in Motion' and 'Personality' and all those things – whereas the band I was trying to get together, we were trying to play the R&B kind of American music that was coming over, more like Little Richard, the Coasters, Chuck Berry, Fats Domino, black artists, not the Pat Boones and the Bobby Vees.

We weren't doing very well, playing youth clubs, doing three or four gigs a week for almost nothing, and my drummer, Tony Chapman, answered an ad from Mick, Keith and Brian in one of the Music papers, and he came back the next day and said, "It's not bad actually, it's a very different kind of music. I've made a tape copy and I thought you'd like to hear it, because they haven't got a bass player either" – it must've been just after Mick Taylor split. So I listened to this stuff, and there were about four or five Jimmy Reed tracks, and I thought it was very interesting and unusual, and it gave me a weird feeling to listen to it, but an excited feeling. But I thought, "It's *so* slow," because we were playing all the uptempo, semi-black stuff. So I said, "All right, I'll go up."

So we went up there, and it was snowing and cold, to this horrible pub where there was a rehearsal hall, and nobody spoke to me for two hours. Mick said hullo to me when I arrived and Stu, who was playing piano, was nice, but Brian and Keith never spoke to me until they found out I had some cigarettes, because they never had any money, so I bought them each a drink and we were all mates. They asked us to join, and our band wasn't doing very well, so we did, but after about three weeks they asked Tony Chapman, who wasn't a very good drummer, if he would leave, and asked Charlie if he would join permanently.

I wasn't involved at all with the jazz thing that was going on in London, or even the R&B thing. I was more into rock 'n roll, rather than the Korner thing, so the whole thing was *very very* strange to me, and it was only Chuck Berry that held me in with the band for the first few weeks, because I knew all those Chuck Berry songs, and I knew Bo Diddley vaguely. I don't know any of the blues people, but at least when they said, let's do 'Reeling and Rocking', I knew it backwards, and doing a blues on the bass was fairly simple anyway. It was just popular music that was being played by black artists instead of white, really, that was the difference, and we suddenly realised it was better.
Bill Wyman, 1978.

I came out of the school that never listened to rock 'n' roll, or refused to until I was about twenty-one. I was never really that good to play what you might term "jazz", particularly at that time, so I just used to play with anyone really, which was mostly jazz people, but not on a very high musical level, not the best, though some of them turned out to be the best as time passed.

When I first played with Cyril Davies in Alexis Korner's band, I thought, "What the fuck is happening here?" because I'd only ever heard harmonica played by Larry Adler, but Cyril was such a character, I loved him. But the rest of it! I didn't know what the hell was going on. Although I knew about playing a heavy backbeat, it wasn't like Chicago, which was what Cyril wanted. Now Alexis never really did front that band, so you had Dick Heckstall-Smith, then Jack Bruce, Graham Bond, Ginger Baker, an amazing band, but a total cacophony of sound. On a good night it was amazing, but it was like a cross between R&B and Charlie Mingus, which was what Alexis wanted.

By the time I joined the Stones, I was a bit used to rock 'n' roll. I knew most of the rock 'n' roll guys, people like Screaming Lord Sutch, through people who played in bands (like Sutch's pianist, Nicky Hopkins), though I never had any desire to play it myself. But by the time I actually joined the Stones, I was quite used to Chuck Berry and that. But it was actually sitting up endlessly with Keith and Brian – I was out of work at the time I joined them and I just used to hang about with them, waiting for jobs to come up, daytime work – just listening to Little Walter and all that, that it got ground in.
Charlie Watts, 1978.

Did you have an idea what you were getting into when you went to that rehearsal?
Well, sort of. . . . The drummer had brought back a tape from that first rehearsal so that I could learn some songs. He played it, and it was so slow and funky. It was a Jimmy Reed tune, actually, and I had never heard the blues before, apart from early jazz-blues things like Jelly Roll Morton. None of that stuff had ever been released in England.
So what made them decide you were the man they were looking for?
By that time I owned a Vox AC-30 amplifier, which was really something in those days. It was like your Fender Twin, if you like, which was quite a valuable asset. So they thought, "Oh, really good amp; bass player's nothing special, but we'll keep him so we can use the amp." That was the general opinion, I have since learned. You know, they are real con artists, that lot.
Bill Wyman, 1978.

So who used to choose the material for the Stones?
We all did. There were certain speciality numbers.
Like "featuring the drummer"?
No. He never wanted to play anything. Charlie never could play a solo, and don't believe him when he says he only joined the band on a temporary basis [laughs] – it was the only gig he could get. Charlie didn't want to join the band because we didn't have any gigs. *Mick Jagger.*

Mick, Keith & Brian.

We were really a team. But there was always something between Brian, Mick and myself that didn't quite make it somewhere. Always something. I've often thought, tried to figure it out. It was in Brian, somewhere, there was some-thing . . . he still felt alone somewhere . . . he was either completely into Mick at the expense of me, like nicking my bread to go and have a drink. Like when I was zonked out, taking the only pound I had in my pocket. He'd do something like that. Or he'd be completely in with me trying to work something against Mick.

Brian was a very weird cat. He was a little insecure. He wouldn't be able to make it with two other guys at one time and really get along well. *Keith Richards.*

At the beginning, there was a tussle between Brian and Mick. That was mainly Brian's hang up, because it just so happened that Mick naturally came to the fore as the band grew from a rhythm and blues club band to a sort of pop mania chart thing.
     Between 1963 and '64, Brian was very hung up about it. Mick was getting all the attention, yet Brian saw himself as the leader. Brian organised it and used to hold the bread after the gigs and pay everybody. But when the band got into the popularity thing, Mick took over and it caused Brian some upset which he never really quite got over. It brought about some other forms of paranoia later. *Keith Richards.*

I went out one morning and came back in the evening and Brian was *blowing harp*, man. He's got it together. He's standin' at the top of the stairs sayin', "Listen to this." *Whooooow. Whoooow.* All these blues notes comin' out. "I've learned how to do it. I've figured it out." One day.
     So then he started to really work on the harp. He dropped the guitar. He still dug to play it and was still into it and played very well but the harp became his thing. He'd walk around all the time playing his harp. *Keith Richards,* 1971.

I never really wanted to be the leader, but somehow I automatically got all the attention. I had the most recognisable features etc., though I didn't really know or care. Brian cared a lot, but it didn't worry me.
     That was the thing that fucked Brian up — because he was desperate for attention. He wanted to be admired and loved and all that . . . which he was by a lot of people, but it wasn't enough for him. *Mick Jagger.*

Keith was my friend from way back, but he was also close to Brian, which was great for the band. However, there were terrible periods when everyone was against Brian, which was stupid, but then on the other hand Brian was a very difficult person to get on with and he didn't help. *Mick Jagger.*

The only incident I can recall wasn't over music. That was when Keith gave Brian a black eye when he ate Keith's meat pie or something. There's been a few little incidents like that. I don't know. . . it's amazing that the band doesn't have those kind of big fights all the time. *Bill Wyman,* 1965.

It was all a very casual thing on the club scene at that time. Korner was doing an awful lot for the music. He was really the only guy doing anything about rhythm and blues in Britain.

Mick and Keith were at school together in London. One day I decided to leave Korner, and I formed a little band that wasn't going very well. I got together with Mick and Keith, and that was the nucleus of the Rolling Stones. *Charlie Watts,* 1964.

Small-Time Gigs.

We were desperate for work. Desperate. First week we played there – 150 people. We thought it was marvellous. We'd all taken the plunge, professionally, and we didn't care how much we got paid, as long as we got a start. Well, it got bigger and bigger. The audiences came from miles around, as they say in the best books. *Mick Jagger,* 1964.

Brian and I were the sort of people they were glad to kick out. They'd say, "You're nothin' but bums, you're gonna end up on skid row," and that sort of thing. Probably will anyway. *Keith Richards,* 1971.

I think our change came about the same time a lot of the beat groups started. When there were no hit groups and the Beatles were playing the Cavern. We were blues purists who liked ever so commercial things but never did them on stage because we were so horrible and so aware of being blues purists, you know what I mean? You see, nobody knew each other in those days. We didn't know the Beatles and the Animals and this and that and the other group, yet we were all doing the same material. We used to be so surprised to hear other people do the same things we were doing. The thing is that the public didn't know about any of this music because the record companies were issuing hundreds of singles a week, so naturally most people missed a huge lot of them. *Mick Jagger.*

Most of these clubs at the time were filled with dixieland bands, traditional jazz bands. An alternative to all that Bobby Vee stuff. There was a big boom in that: the stomp, stomping about, weird dance, just really trying to break the ceiling to a

two beat. That was the big scene. They had all the clubs under control. That's where Alexis [Korner] made the breakthrough. He managed to open it up at the Ealing club. Then he moved on to the Marquee and R&B started to become the thing. And all these traddies, as they were called, started getting worried. So they started this very bitter opposition. *Keith Richards.*

I can remember buying Barrett Strong's 'Money', which was a really big R&B hit in America, but didn't happen when it came out in England. When we saw that those things were popular, we said, well, let's do that. So we did. *Mick Jagger.*

When we went into the ballrooms in the autumn of '63, we found out that you couldn't play such things as those slow Jimmy Reed blues type numbers. You were expected to play more for them to dance to, but they never danced. Instead they just stood there in front of you and gaped.

So at that time, we started concentrating on much more uptempo songs, fast rhythm things, hard rockers which seemed to work out quite well. So you couldn't always stick to the original even if you wanted to. But there was also another thing. If you admire a particular artist and the great sound that he gets on his records you can find yourself in the position where you can't think of any other treatment that's going to improve it, because what's on the record is as good as it's ever going to be. So you just have to try and get as close to the record as possible. *Bill Wyman.*

What were the kind of things that were a problem when you were starting out?
Oh, things like having to wear the same sweaty shirt three nights running. Is it two short sets or one long set? Or else Brian's hidden half the money from the gig under the carpet, and you find it . . . [in very innocent voice] "Oh you mean that money, I was saving it for guitar strings."

Basically, it was learning to handle our own egos. When the first singles were happening, you could feel the changes taking place, feel the pressure building up.

I was nineteen when it started to take off, right, and just a very ordinary guy.

MICK JAGGER 1963/DEZO HOFFMAN

Chucked out of nightclubs, birds' 'd poke their tongues out at me, that kind of scene.

And then suddenly, Adonis! And, you know, that is *so* ridiculous, so totally insane.

It makes you very cynical. But it's a hell of a thing to deal with. It really is a bugger.

Looking back now, happily married man an' all that, it seems incredibly funny, but it took me years to get it under control. *Keith Richards.*

The Start Of Stardom.

When did you realise that it might be possible to make a living out of music?

At the time I didn't have any idea of how I was going to make a living. I remember the first time I played with Alexis·Korner I made a pound or ten bob.

What about the story that you didn't broadcast with Alexis because the Stones had a booking on the same night?

That's a lie. Alexis had a band and Charlie was the drummer. He had this BBC broadcast which was a big deal – but instead of having Charlie, who was in the band, he got someone else because he said Charlie wasn't a professional musician, 'cause he had some other job as well.

I didn't really expect to go on the broadcast because I was only one of his singers . . . Alexis used to sing, so did Cyril (Davies), Long John Baldry, Ronnie Jones, Paul Jones. But the thing is, we didn't have any gigs at all. We had a gig that night but it was one that Alexis had given us. I think that must have been our very first gig.

I can remember seeing you at The Marquee when the band was billed as Mick Jagger and Brian Jones and The Rolling Stones. Was this indicative of a joint leadership?

We only played down The Marquee about half-a-dozen times. As to who was the leader. . . Well, Brian used to want to be, but nobody really wanted to be the leader of the band – it seemed a rather outmoded idea.

Even though we were all working together Brian desperately wanted to be the leader, but nobody ever accepted him as such. I don't mean within the band. I mean with the kids. Up until then it'd been accepted by the public that the singer with the band was the leader and, as I just happened to be the singer, most people automatically singled me out as the leader.

Brian used to really get upset . . . I didn't give a shit who was the leader of the band. I mean, I don't want to be the leader of the band now, let alone then.

Who was looking after the business side of the band at that time?

The first cat we had who looked after the band was Giorgio Gomeisky. He was a kind person was Giorgio, because we really didn't care about anybody – just took advantage of everybody. We thought everybody was against us.

What made you think that?

Well, they *were*, basically. We were very hard to get on with – very proud. We knew we were good and we *were*. . . For the time we were *very* good.

There was just nobody else doing it. If Giorgio put us on in front of an audience we used to make them go crazy in two numbers, but there were other people who used to get really uptight and make things difficult. We were booked as the interval band and we made it tough for the band who had to go on after us – the same old story.

You see, we knew we were good because of the crowd reaction, but still we couldn't get any gigs whatsoever. If we did get any gigs. We didn't hang around that long, but at one point we did have a very bad time when we just couldn't get a gig it always used to go very very well and because of this we couldn't understand why nobody would book us.

It was nothing but professional jealousy. Nobody wanted a band looking like us and playing what we wanted to play, because they couldn't understand anyone wanting to hear it. *Mick Jagger, 1974.*

There's only so far you can go on that London scene; if you stay in that club circuit eventually you get constipated. You go round and round so many times and then suddenly, you're not the hip band anymore, someone else is. Like The High Numbers they took over from us in a lot of clubs. The High Numbers turned out to become The Who. The Yardbirds took over from us in Richmond and on Sunday nights we'd find we were booked into a place in Manchester.

It was difficult the first few months though. We were known in the big cities but when you get outside into the sticks, they don't know who the fuck you are and they're still preferring the local band. That makes you play your ass off every night so that at the end of two hour-long sets, you've got 'em.

You've gotta do it. That's the testing ground, in those ballrooms where it's really hard to play. Brian at that time is the leader of the band. He pulled us all together, he's playing good guitar but his love is the harmonica. On top of that, he's got the pop star hangup – he wants to sing, with Mick, like 'Walking the Dog'.

It's weird. I can remember. You know it in front. Being on the road every night you can tell by the way the gigs are going, there's something enormous coming. You can feel this energy building up as you go around the country. You feel it winding tighter and tighter, until one day you get out there halfway through the first number and the whole stage is full of chicks screaming "Nyeehhh". There was a period of six months in England we couldn't play ballrooms anymore because we never got through more than three or four songs every night, man. Chaos. Police and too many people in the places, fainting. We'd walk into some of those places and it was like they had the Battle of the Crimea going on, people gasping, tits hanging out, chicks choking, nurses running around with ambulances.

I know it was the same for the Beatles. One had been reading about that, 'Beatlemania'. 'Scream power' was the thing everything was judged by, as far as gigs were concerned. If Gerry and the Pacemakers were the top of the bill, incredible, man. You know that weird sound that thousands of chicks make when they're really lettin' it go. They couldn't hear the music. We couldn't hear ourselves, for years. Monitors were unheard of. It was impossible to play as a band on stage, and we forgot all about it. *Keith Richards,* 1971.

For us a rave starts pretty quietly. As we drive into town, we stop to ask someone the way to the ballroom. We like to case the joint first, to see how big the crowd is outside. If it looks large and a bit mad, we shoot off to a phone box and lay on an emergency service.

Police and officials bundle us through a secret door. With a bit of luck, our car remains unscratched and unlipsticked, our clothes stay in one piece and we still have as much hair as we started with.

We wander round backstage to scout out the scene. Already we can hear the screams.

"What's the audience like" we ask.

1964

BELLE VUE, MANCHESTER 1964/CONWAY

"Wild!" someone says. And that's great, because that's how we like it.

. . . Standing in the wings, waiting for the curtains to part, you get your first real glimpse of all the excitement. Stage hands frantically beat off girls who are trying to wrench back the stage drapes.

The atmosphere is more than electric by now – it's something tangible, like a vast elastic band, ready to snap at any moment!

And then we're off. Keith roars in to 'Talkin' About You'. The curtains slowly part. The Stones are rolling!

As our music gains momentum, the kids sway like palm trees in a hurricane. A huge Hampden roar swamps our overworked amplifiers. We feel as if we're really in there with the fans.

As the excitement mounts, the girls surge down to the footlights and start showering us with gifts – sweets, peanuts, cuddly toys. We're feeling very good.

Suddenly it's all over. The curtains close quickly, shutting off the faces behind

that ear-splitting roar.

　　Back in the dressing room, we swallow Cokes to get that sandpaper taste out of our throats. We start to unwind as we wait for the police to arrange our getaway. *Brian Jones,* 1964.

Gigs we were turning up to do we couldn't *get in*, let alone play. And if we had've got in, we'd never've got out, so we gave up. And we could easily have become a studio band, couldn't we, Charlie? *Bill Wyman,* 1978.

In a place like Birkenhead, say, we'd go out and start, "I'm gonna tell you how it's gonna be . . . ," three bars and unnnnnh, they'd come sweepin' all over the stage and finished . . . back in the hotel with a thousand quid. Girls leapin' from forty foot balconies and arrows in the paper next day showin' where she jumped from . . . *Bill Wyman,* 1971.

The Boys In The Band.

The Stones just roll on, by their own volition. Not by anybody else's volition. We've not had a manager for years. Can't bear them. *Mick Jagger,* 1977.

What do you think about the future of the Stones?
I don't think I feel any differently about it – as far as I know, it is just going to go on because it feels good to go on right now... if someone is unable to be with the others for a while, then there will just be a gap, but it will go on. I mean, Charlie was getting better and better, man, you just can't let that go, when things are improving all the time for the band. In its own perverse way, we all feel it's getting better. I mean there was a time when nobody thought an act could last more than two years, especially at that point when we started out. I mean, Muddy Waters has just put out a great new album. There is no reason that rock 'n' roll *has* to be played by *adolescents* and *juveniles.* It still feels better from this end. You know, Fred McDowell, all my favourite cats, kept on playing till they dropped, seventy or eighty years old. It's like wine, man, they just get better. *Keith Richards,* 1977.

I'll be keeping it up until my body starts to fall apart and that's a long time off. The Stones might not last for ever but we'll be going until sometime this side of ever. *Mick Jagger,* 1974.

Come to think of it, maybe the reason why the Stones are still going is because we've always been sufficiently aware of what's going on to be influenced, but not so that we slavishly follow trends. *Mick Jagger,* 1974.

Not amazed that the band is still going, just amazed they get anything together. That's our claim to fame, y'know. Carry on lads, regardless. Should be the title of our next film. We're a terrible... band, really. But we are the *oldest.* That's some sort of distinction, innit? Especially in this country. The only difference between us and Westminster Abbey, y'know, is we don't do weddings and coronations. Sometimes I feel like George Lewis. Yes, I know he's dead. Thanks. You know I never did get into George Lewis much. Ed Hall, now he was my favourite – on the liquorice. *Charlie Watts,* 1970.

People overestimate the Rolling Stones. I don't think the Stones are as good as people think. Obviously I think the Stones are a very good band. *Mick Jagger,* 1976.

I never question myself or the Stones too closely; I've always done things on a very instinctive basis, you know. I think brains have gotten in the way of too many things and especially something as basic as what we're doing. You can think about what everybody says about you, good or bad, but it doesn't make any difference to what is going to come out on tape eventually. That's not to say we do any of it without thought, but there's a fine line between something that's worked out and something that's lost that very immediate first take thing. *Keith Richards,* 1977.

The Stones are pretty worldly characters and a lot can bounce off them. If I turned round and slagged them off they could just as easily do without me but I did feel more wanted with them, which is good. I felt needed. There are a lot of lap dogs around the Faces tours. *Ron Wood,* 1976.

Nobody in this band can be persuaded to do something unless he wants to do it. Charlie Watts hates going on the road, but he likes it enough to still pack his suitcase. He only ever carries a hold-all with a change of clothes in it, because he likes to pretend he's going to go home the next day. *Keith Richards,* 1979.

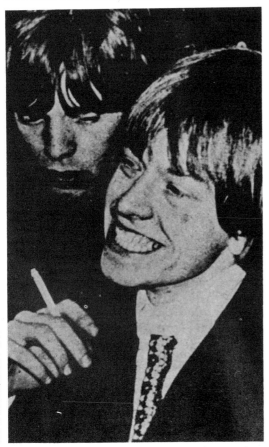

BRIAN JONES, MICK JAGGER 1965

It's easier having someone else alongside you in the driver's seat taking care of his side of the scheme while you take care of your part. And of course there's that chemistry thing there too . . . *Mick Jagger.*

Bob Dylan was by himself. With us there's always been someone there to grip the reins when it's necessary. *Keith Richards.*

No, I am not apart. I am one-fifth of the Rolling Stones. We are essentially a group. We have fun at concerts, always have a laugh. No, I'm not deserted, lonely or apart on stage. *Mick Jagger.*

With the Faces Rod used to tighten up the reins if the band was getting a bit loose. It's the exact opposite with Mick, because he'll go and sit at the piano and fumble around during my guitar solos. Rod used to inhibit me. *Ron Wood, 1976.*

It must be something about us to make them think this is it, this is the epitome. I can't go beyond this. If I can do this with the Stones I can do it with anybody, which is bullshit. Mick and I know that. We can write a song for the Stones and do it right but we can write a song and throw it around to various people, they get nowhere. It's just a matter of realising your limitations. *That's* why we've outlasted everyone else. *Keith Richards.*

Blues For Brian.

Such a beautiful cat, man. He was one of those people who are so beautiful in one way, and such an asshole in another. "Brian, how could you do that to me, man?" It was like that. *Keith Richards.*

When I first met Brian he was in the process of getting a band together and moving up to London with one of his many women and children. God knows how many he had. He sure left his mark, that cat. I know of five kids, at least. All by different chicks, and they all look like Brian. *Keith Richards, 1971.*

We haven't changed during these past months when it has all happened for us. It's the public – they've come to understand what we're getting at, and after a long time have decided they like it. We had enough hard times, with people laughing up their sleeves at us, and we were the ones who had to show real determination. I used bottleneck guitar, for instance. Nobody knew what was going on. The harmonica bits, in the early days, had people baffled.

We get letters now from groups asking us what they should do to make a name for themselves. Some even ask us exactly how we go about getting our sound. Well, we've learned those lessons for ourselves and it all adds up to finding the sort of music you most want to do . . . and having the guts to stick with it. If you don't believe in yourselves, you won't get anywhere.

About the money bit. We know that money is important. But we're in this business principally because we enjoy it, because we get pleasure out of it. Cut off the money and you'll still find us playing this kind of music . . . even if we have to go back to bumming drinks off people to keep going. You can tell the phonies a mile off. And the worst part of it all is that they are the ones who do the loudest shouting about us. *Brian Jones, 1966.*

Around '66 I had a change of heart because the pressure dropped off as we stopped touring; for the next year Brian and I became firm friends again — I was living with him and Anita for two years. The thing that blew it was when we went down to Morocco and he was pulling this hard man number knocking off Moroccan whores — ugh — and being absolutely disgusting and everything, so I said, "Come on baby, I'm taking you home", so we left and that was the end of Brian and me as friends.

Over that year I'd developed a very strong friendship. I'd managed to break down a lot of barriers, but you see Brian always had to have an imaginary foe. He was a bit of a Don Quixote, I suppose. Brian would always manipulate people into these situations of proving your friendship to him by doing something dastardly to the other person.

All I tried to do with Brian was bring him more into the groove because he wasn't really doing anything any more, he wasn't contributing anything to the group. All I wanted to do was bring him back into the mainstream again, but Brian used that fact to create a vendetta against Mick, because Brian always wanted to be . . . like this whole thing of, "Who do the chicks like most?", that started with him back in '63.
Keith Richards.

Brian often appeared to be the odd one out in the triangle which you and he and Keith made up. Unable to relate simultaneously to both of you.

There was a lot of that. Three's a crowd – which is a teenage situation. Nevertheless it was very true.

Keith was my friend from way back, but he was also close to Brian, which was great for the band. However, there were terrible periods when everyone was against Brian which was stupid but then on the other hand Brian was a very difficult person to get on with and he didn't help.
Mick Jagger, 1974.

Our real followers have moved on with us — some of those we like most are the hippies in New York, but nearly all of them think like us and are questioning some of the basic immoralities which are tolerated in present day society — the war in Vietnam, persecution of homosexuals, illegality of abortion, drug taking. All these things are immoral. We are making our own statement — others are making more intellectual ones.

Our friends are questioning the wisdom of an almost blind acceptance of religion compared with total disregard for reports related to things like unidentified flying objects which seem more real to me. Conversely I don't underestimate the power or influence of those, unlike me, who do believe in God.

We believe there can be no evolution without revolution. I realise there are other inequalities — the ratio between affluence and reward for work done is all wrong. I know I earn too much but I'm still young and there's something spiteful inside me which makes me want to hold on to what I've got.

I believe we're moving toward a new age in ideas and events. Astrologically we are at the end of the age called the Pisces age — at the beginning of which people like Christ were born. We're soon to begin the age of Aquarius, in which events as important as those at the beginning of Pisces are likely to occur. There's a young revolution in thought and manner about to take place.
Brian Jones, 1967.

Brian got very fragile. As he went along, he got more and more fragile and delicate. His personality and physically. I think all that touring did a lot to break him. We worked our asses off from '63 to '66 right through those three years, nonstop. I believe we had two weeks off. That's nothing, I mean I tell that to B.B. King and he'll say, "I've been doing it for years". But for cats like Brian . . . He was tough but one thing and another he slowly became more fragile. When I first met Brian he was like a little Welsh bull. He was broad, and he seemed to be very tough.

For a start, people were always laying stuff on him because he was a Stone. And he'd try it. He'd take anything. Any other sort of trip too, head trips. He never had time to work it out 'cause we were on the road all the time, always on the plane the next day. Eventually, it caught up. *Keith Richards.*

Such psychic weaklings has Western civilisation made of so many of us.
Brian Jones, 1969.

I mean, Brian gradually gave up all interest in the guitar, he just wouldn't touch it – so it would be down to me to lay down all the guitar tracks while he would be leaping around on the dulcimer or the marimba. I never really thought about it then, I just did it. *Keith Richards.*

Trouble In Paradise.

We were sitting on the ground with Brian, under the very low eaves of this thatched farm house, and the musicians were working just four or five feet away, ahead of us in the court-yard where the animals usually are. It was getting to be time to eat, and suddenly two of the musicians came along with a snow-white goat. The goat disappeared off into the shadows with the two musicians, one of whom was holding a long knife which Brian suddenly caught the glitter of, and he started to get up, making a sort of funny noise, and he said, "That's me!" And everybody picked up on it right at once and said, yeah, right, it looks just like you. It was perfectly true, he had this fringe of blond hair hanging right down in front of his eyes, and we said, of course that's you. Then about twenty minutes later we were eating this goat's liver on shish-kebab sticks. *Keith Richards,* 1971.

Like Jimi Hendrix. He just couldn't suss the assholes from the good people. He wouldn't kick out somebody that was a shit. He'd let them sit there and maybe they'd be thinking how to sell off his possessions. He'd give them booze and he'd feed them and they'd be thinking, "Oh, that's worth 250 quid and I can roll that up and take it away". I don't know. *Keith Richards.*

I'm very hung up on electronic music at present. If there's not room to include it on our album I would like to do something separately. *Brian Jones,* 1967.

The Stones' music is not to my taste any more. I want to play my own kind of music. Their music has progressed at a tangent to my own musical tastes. *Brian Jones,* 1968.

I was invited to do a session with the Stones. It puzzled me. I had never met Mick Jagger in my life and here he was phoning me.
  I went down and played on some

tracks and thought little more about it. Then they asked me if I wanted to be a Stone. I was amazed. Brian Jones was leaving, I was told. I said I'd love to be a Stone and that was that. *Mick Taylor,* 1969.

Brian just seemed to deteriorate over the last couple of years of his life. So he wasn't that much of a loss, musically, around that time. When Mick Taylor took over he kind of gave us a little booster. *Bill Wyman.*

We'd known for a few months that Brian wasn't keen, he wasn't enjoying himself, and it got to the stage where we had to sit down and talk about it. So we did and we decided the best thing was for Brian to leave. *Mick Jagger.*

We were at a session that night and we weren't expecting Brian to come along. He'd officially left the band. We were doing the first gig with Mick Taylor that night. No, I wouldn't say that was true. Maybe Mick had been with us for a week or so but it was very close to when Mick had joined. And someone called us up at midnight and said, "Brian's dead".
  Well, what the fuck's going on? We had these chauffeurs working for us and we tried to find out . . . some of them had a weird hold over Brian. There were a lot of chicks there and there was a whole thing going on, they were having a party. I don't know, man, I just don't know what happened to Brian that night.
  There was no one there that'd want to murder him. Somebody didn't take care of him. And they should have done because he had somebody there who was supposed to take care of him. Everyone knew what Brian was like, especially at a party. Maybe he did just go in for a swim and have an asthma attack. I'd never seen Brian have an attack. I know that he was asthmatic. I know that he was hung up with his spray but I've never seen him have an attack. He was a good swimmer. He was a better swimmer than anybody else around me. He could dive off those rocks straight into the sea.
  He was really easing back from the whole drug thing. He wasn't hitting them like he had been, he wasn't hitting anything like he had. Maybe the combination of things. It's one of those things I just can't find out. You know, who do you ask? *Keith Richards.*

How much of a vacuum did Brian leave in the band?

We weren't playing, that was the thing, but we were recording a lot of good material on our own, the four of us.

Brian played on some of 'Beggar's Banquet' – not all of it. Let's say he was helpful. I don't know exactly how many tracks he played on but that was his album. We did 'Let it Bleed' without him.

But Brian wasn't around towards the end. What we didn't like was that we wanted to play again on stage and Brian wasn't in any condition to play. He couldn't play. He was far too fucked up in his mind to play.

Surely this must have affected the morale of the Stones?

It did. We felt like we had a wooden leg. We wanted to go out and play but Brian couldn't. I don't think that he really wanted to and it was this that really pissed me off. He didn't have any desire to go on stage and play. *Mick Jagger, 1974.*

[The Stones concert in Hyde Park, July 5 1969. Brian died two days before.]
Brian would have wanted it to go on. We will do the concert for Brian. I hope people will understand that it is because of our love for him that we are still doing it. *Mick Jagger, 1969.*

HYDE PARK, 1969

Right now, I'm sticking pretty much to playing rhythm on stage. It depends on the number usually, but since Brian died I've had to pay more attention to rhythm guitar anyway. I move more now simply because back when we were playing old halls I had to stand next to Charlie's drums in order to catch the beat, the sound was always so bad.
Keith Richards, 1970.

How long did it take to achieve the degree of co-ordination that you and Mick Taylor demonstrate?

Uh. . . difficult question. Y'see, ever since the first night he came along, it's been a turn-on to play with him. Looking back now, we weren't half as good, say, two years ago, as we are now, and we're improving all the time.

Live, we swap roles all the time. It's more than just rhythm and lead, and it's really liberated me – having Mick there.

Like I was playin' with Brian for years,

and when Brian got disinterested with guitar, suddenly the whole load fell on me, and I really didn't dig that at all.

I find it hard to get off when I have to carry the thing, with just bass and drums in support. I much prefer two guitars, three if possible. . . four, five. . . six! Why not?

On stage I can't really hear what Mick's playing. All I can hear is a vague echo – I'm right over the other side of the stage. So I have to feel my way into it. I'm usually pleasantly surprised when I hear tapes of performances. *Keith Richards.*

Did Mick Taylor give you any indication he was thinking of quitting?

No. Nothing. What pisses me off is not that he wanted to leave. It's the *way* he left. We're getting ready to cut our next album [*It's Only Rock 'n' Roll*], the sessions and everything were already planned out. We all met in Geneva three weeks ago to talk about the album, we booked time at Musicland [studios in Munich], discussed our upcoming tour of the States. Never once did he voice any doubts about continuing with the group. He seemed OK, y'know. He obviously had a lot of 'troubles' – personal problems that are nothing to do with us or the press. I don't honestly know the true nature of them, but there you go. Yeah, I suppose it was a bit inconsiderate of him to inform us a day before we were about to enter the studios but . . . maybe he hadn't made up his mind until that point. I was in Managua, Nicaragua, at the time checking out on how the benefit was doing when I received a call from the office that Mick Taylor wasn't coming to the Munich sessions. Then I received a call saying Mick Taylor wasn't going anywhere anymore with the Stones.

So . . . well, I couldn't really discuss the whys and wherefores on a telephone line between Nicaragua and London with Mick, so I flew back to London. We went to the Clapton concert together and then a party at Robert Stigwood's and had a heart-to-heart there and everything.

He just said "Yeah, I'd like to leave the group", and I said "Fine", y'know. He seemed a bit unsure . . . I mean, he obviously wanted to do something else but then again it's a bit of a gamble. I am, however, *very very* disappointed that he's leaving because he's such a great musician. Also . . . I hope, and I don't see why anyway, but . . . I'm still going to socialise

with him and everything because I do like him a lot and we used to hang out together a lot. We always get on very well on tours.

The contention that Keith might carry on as the sole guitarist for the Stones even in an on-stage capacity . . . ?

Oh, that's bullshit! Keith would only ever conceive of doing that for maybe one gig if someone was sick. I mean, we'd go on but . . . Christ, Keith wouldn't want to do that and I *certainly wouldn't* [laughs].

Yeah, I know that he played pretty much all by himself back in '66 when Brian was too out of it, but *then* we only had to do twenty minutes and everyone was screaming so you couldn't hear anything anyway.

Nobody listened and I'd just jump up in the air a couple of times and that was it. Now you actually have to play [laughs].

Uh, Mick, do the words "Ron Wood" mean anything to you at this particular juncture? After all speculation is rife.

It would have been nice if Ron had come down for the sessions here, y'know, but he's touring at the moment. I don't know about permanently finding someone. It's going to take a little while. In the meantime, I want to play with a lot of people and by that, I'm not trying to be evasive but . . . ah on record there's a lot of people I could dig working with.

I've played with Ron a lot. I had one very good night playing with Jeff Beck recently. There's Eric [Clapton] too. They're all great friends of mine. As far as finding a permanent guy, I really don't know at the moment simply because I haven't had time to think about it.

But the image of the Stones as a four-piece. That's going to be weird but at the same time, is it going to be worth it to actually graft in another full-time fledgling à la Mick Taylor's appearance in '69?

I'd like to find another one sure. We've got to find another, for Chrissakes. For this tour which is going to take place in America in May, though I don't know if I should tell you that because it's best to keep these things a secret because you get all these arseholes bothering you and stuff.

Back to Taylor though. Do you ever feel that he got upset about that constant undercurrent of media burbling concerning him not being a true Rolling Stone.

Well, I think if he'd been the kind of guy who'd got himself a really bad reputation and had got himself busted all

NEW YORK 1979/MICHAEL PUTLAND/LFI

the time then all those people would have been saying – "Yeah, he's a real Rolling Stone, blah, blah" which is bullshit! You don't have to behave like an idiot to be part of a band. That's what they really meant.

I mean as far as the music's concerned he fitted in, and as far as living together he fitted in, simply because he didn't get into trouble. Which is something I consider to be supremely sensible. No-one wants all that hassle – with all those stupid newspapers.

Now if we had John Lennon in the band [laughs] – or someone like that . . . if Keith Moon came in and played guitar – God forbid – well you can imagine that! I mean, I thought Mick fitted in perfectly, instantly in fact.

Without the horn section and without Mick [Taylor] – who both curiously departed at the same time, the Stones sound similar to that brash rhythmic arrogance that earned us our reputation in the beginning. The songs sound a lot rougher now and I think that's got a lot to do with Ronnie. He's a more basic guitar player, more rhythmic. There's not as many pretty solos but the playing is more *gutsy!* And that does help because we are that sort of band.

Taylor did great things with the band, great things on guitar. Neither one is better but change is nice. When Taylor joined it was a change for the better and so is the addition of Ronnie. Change always turns you on to new things.

Even in these early infant stages, Ron Wood fits?

If something goes wrong Ronnie has to run over and kind of suss out what's going on. He doesn't know Keith that well yet. If he plays with us long enough he will do. But he's got his own band and he's got his solo career. It's nice to have him on tour but I don't know about the future. *Bill Wyman,* 1975.

A Certain Chemistry.

There's something to be said for a certain chemistry between people that makes for a certain kind of music.

It must be obvious from the way the Beatles have split up and what's happened since. Although they're very good individually, no matter how much they say how little they worked together as a band, they did work together. 'Cause nothing they've done since has surpassed that. *Keith Richards.*

What am I doing? I'm with these blokes till August 14th, then I go straight out with the Faces, then with these guys again.

Then I have a decision to make!

Where it changed, they were looking around and looking around and finally said, "Look, we aren't gonna do the tour if you don't do it." So I said, well, it's serious then, is it? I'd known all along that I'd like to do it, but I hadn't dared to think about it too long. Same as they hadn't, because they like our band as much as we like theirs. And I always think of the Faces before I do anything. But I thought, well, they can't blame me, really.
Ron Wood, 1975.

Keith and Ron are both brilliant rhythm guitar players. 'E's fun on the road. That's what it's all about, innit? I heard the Average White Band rehearsed a thousand drummers before making a choice, but, Christ it's not like you're hiring a cook or something. Know what I mean?
Mick Jagger, 1975.

Personally, if you want to know my opinion, I think the split's a very good thing. The Stones are *together* again. 'United' could be the word. And it's just like old times. Really, it is. Before Mick was in the band, I mean, I think Mick is a great musician and I liked him as a bloke but he wasn't one of The Rolling Stones. His sound was different.

I mean, Keith's guitar sound *is* the Stones sound, right–absolutely, yeah –and Mick had a different sound and approach and its very presence obviously changed that Stones sound to some degree . . . I think for the worse.

I don't honestly think the split could have come at a better time. I mean, the Stones have used him and got what they wanted out of him and he's done himself a lot of good with the Stones. I'm really looking forward to hearing what Mick will come up with, y'know.

How have the Stones taken it? Well, obviously they've taken it in different ways, but still they're all pretty upset, because they *did* like him as a bloke as well as a musician. That's another thing. He fitted in pretty well as a personality. But then as he grew more confident he started to exert more of himself into the Stones music and . . . personally I don't think it was for the better. I repeat, though, that this is all based on purely selfish motivation because . . . well, it is like old times, I feel.

I mean, the Stones have improved in the studio. I suppose . . . but w-e-e-ll, it's always the same thing. Some nights they're beautiful, other nights they're diabolical.
Ron Wood, 1975.

I was very happy with what came out [*Black and Blue* album] personally. I thought Wayne Perkins was great. He's a lovely guitar player but he's too much like Mick Taylor in one respect. It would have been lovely to have him but he was American and we had to own up we were an English rock band. It became so obvious when Ronnie walked into the studio. *Keith Richards.*

This band I'm enjoying more than any since the first five basic Rolling Stones.

Ron's presence enables us to take the group back much more to what it originally set out to do. What two guitars are supposed to do. Mick Taylor's a lovely guitar player but there's no way he can get out of that syndrome of being a lead guitar. That's what was good about Brian, in the early days before he lost interest. *Keith Richards.*

Yeah, I'm a Rolling Stone now. I'd like to devote a lot of time to it now. I suppose I could go off at a tangent but I'd like to pile some energy into the Stones for a while and see what comes out. I wasn't involved with 'Black and Blue' from the beginning and I'd just like to see how an album would turn out if I was involved from the start. *Ron Wood,* 1976.

Mick Taylor and I are two different kettles of fish. I tend to open up the nonsense side combined with getting down to good music whereas Mick was good music and seriousness. And they've realised that they really didn't dig that when I came around. *Ron Wood,* 1975.

With Mick Taylor, the role of the guitar player was very fixed because Mick plays *lead* solos and I play rhythm. Because Mick is that kind of guitar player you'll never get the kind of thing you get with Ronnie which is throwing it around between us. It's not that one is better but this is more fun. I prefer it this way because I don't like rigidly *defined* rules for playing. I don't agree that so and so is a *lead* guitar and so and so is a rhythm guitar. We're all just guitar players. Playing with Ronnie is a lot more how. . . how Brian and I started. The idea of two guitars and what they should do. *Keith Richards,* 1975.

I'll tell you where my influence really paid off, though, on *Some Girls*: giving Mick guitar lessons. I encouraged him to play things like 'Respectable', 'Lies', 'When the Whip Comes Down' – all that upbeat, punky stuff. Mick felt very punky at the time. *Ron Wood,* 1979.

We'll stay onstage for a long time – that's where we feel alive the most. I never want just to make records. That's like being a movie or TV actor – you're never doing it in front of a real audience. I couldn't stand that. You could be seen by millions of people every day and still be the loneliest person in the world. *Ron Wood,* 1979.

Woody's come along and, especially in the last year – I noticed it more than anything when we started recording for the new album – he's pulled both sides together, and I think he was the main reason for the band being so close and super friendly in, say, the last nine months than we've been since, I don't know, '66 maybe. Really being able to talk to each other. I found great difficulty after a while in being able to communicate, basically with Mick and Keith. I never had a problem with Charlie, never had a problem with Mick Taylor or Brian, but Woody's really pulled us all in, because . . . I don't know, he talks to Mick and Keith and Charlie, and it's all very amusing and lighthearted – he's always joking – and he can always make you laugh. *Bill Wyman.*

The Stones are very inspiring to play with because they don't have any restrictions. *Ron Wood,* 1976.

Grandfathers Of Pop.

It does get boring people asking me, "Is this the last Stones tour?" They been askin' that since 1964. *Mick Jagger,* 1976.

Ugh, it's 'orrible, to be the Grand Old Men. If all this talk gets any worse I'll be getting another band.
I dunno why, but it's not nice to be asked that question. It makes us sound like survivors from a holocaust.
I s'pose I should be grateful that I survived the Swinging Blue Jeans era, but that was the era before us I always believed. I never felt I was part of it, the Swinging Blue Jeans and that, doing me top twenty hits every evenin' on stage. Whenever I used to see them play they were just all *them,* standing in line together, doing their hits. I think they were something else. We played in a different way. *Mick Jagger,* 1971.

I'm not boring, [grins]. Sure I'm visually boring. I don't think I'd dig watching Chuck Berry just stand there. But I don't like to see someone moving about who doesn't naturally do it as some bands do. People always say I just stand there, dreaming away, not paying any attention but it isn't that at all. I'm right there into every moment. It's just that I don't sweat, [sly grin]. I just get mental strain whereas Keith and Mick probably get both.
People don't realise how much effort is involved. If they don't see you doing a Little Richard on top of the piano they think either you're not into it or you're being lazy. But some people just aren't onstage movers. Yet another example of the band's uncanny ability to realise group and individual limitations and not to exceed them. *Bill Wyman.*

So what do you want to do to keep from getting bored again?
Actually, I've been working on an idea for a film score lately. I'd like to do some electronic music. Nothing heavy or complicated, but something very simple. I've got a Polymoog and an ARP synthesizer that I've been using to put some things down on a 4-track. What I'm looking for is a chance to write descriptive music for a visual thing. I got turned on by all those spaghetti westerns by Sergio Leone, and they got me trying to write descriptive music. I've got quite hung up on that in the last year or so, and I'd like to experiment with it some more with some new instruments just to see what happens. That's really my next goal. Now all I need to do is find a film maker who will trust in me. *Bill Wyman,* 1978.

Bill has the biggest bladder in existence. When he gets going you don't move for fifteen minutes. *Keith Richards.*

[When asked why he didn't sing more songs . . .]
What the hell would Mick do?
Keith Richards, 1971.

WITH GENE PITNEY AND PHIL SPECTOR, 1964

I give the impression of being bored, but I'm not really. I've just got an incredibly boring face. *Charlie Watts.*

Life'd be very tricky if I didn't have a car. *Charlie Watts.*

I haven't been on a tour yet where I was bored. At the end of the last American tour we began to look around for dates, because for us it's just starting to get good. Because this is a new band for us. It's only the second tour but it's got a lot more fire. The last band [he says with suitable distaste] was too intellectual. *Keith Richards,* 1977.

Most bands who started around the same time as you have either returned to obscurity or are now appearing on Rock Revival Shows.
Well, it can't go on for ever. The thing that bugs me is that I get treated like The Grandfather Of Pop, just like James Brown is regarded as The Grandfather of Soul – and I do get treated like that. Now, I'm only three years older than David Bowie. Or is it two?
I don't know why we've kept going. I think really because we were successful. But that's sorta begging the question. The reason we were successful was because of something else.

Do you think the Rolling Stones still appeal to a teenage audience?
Aw, I don't have to do everything twice! We don't have to go back to those people. [Sardonically] Why, some of our audience even here are much younger than I am. Many of the kids who dig us in America are fifteen years old. Christ, in Italy they're nine! Here it's students. That's why I'm not interested in going back to small English towns and turning on the ten-year-olds. I've been and done all that.
We've always had a much older audience than that here anyway. We played to the Richmond art school lot, and they were eighteen to twenty-one. I've always considered our audience to be students, and that's who was there when we played Manchester, Newcastle and the rest on that English tour last year. *Mick Jagger,* 1971.

I'm bored with rock 'n' roll. *Mick Jagger,* 1972.

Sure we know our limitations. Most bands know their limitations but they try and exceed them, pretend the limitations don't exist. I know I'm not the world's greatest bass player and I'm quite happy knowing that. I don't try and fool anybody. It's enough for me to know I'm competent. I've got no big ego. I know I'm not Jack Bruce. Great if you are but I'm not. *Bill Wyman.*

I get bored anywhere. The only time I'm not bored is when I'm drawing, playing the drums or talking. I talk a lot, about nothing usually, and all contradictory. Shirley always accuses me of having no beliefs. Maybe that's why I can talk to anyone. *Charlie Watts.*

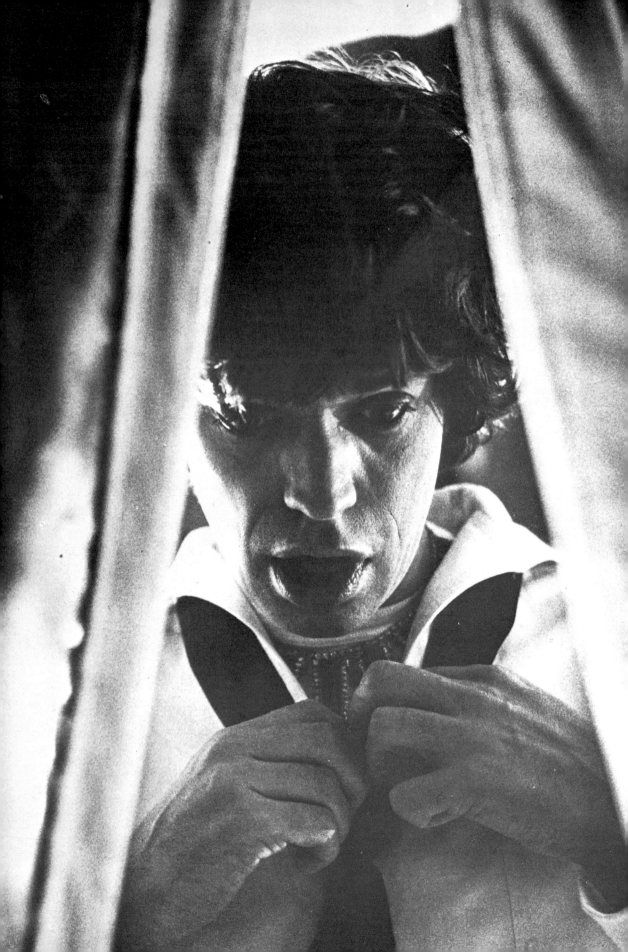

Performance.

Well, I'm so f-f-glad to be here tonight, so glad to be in your wonderful town, yes, and I got a message tonight for everybody that ever needed somebody to love – love 'em *all* the time, when you're up and when you're down. Yeah, babe, some time you thinking you getting what you want, then you go and lose what you had, but don't despair just take it easy now, listen to my song tonight and save the whole world – ah, yeah . . . *Mick Jagger,* (on stage).

"Self-employed entertainer" it says on my passport. *Keith Richards, 1976.*

I'm a dedicated show-business person. I'll go onstage and do Noel Coward. I mean, I'm just a show-business person, whether it's playing guitar, piano, acting, singing, dancing. I just chose rock 'n' roll as my career in show business. If I'd been born in 1915, I'd have been a jazz drummer or singer in a jazz band or an actor. *Mick Jagger, 1978.*

Sure, but I'm cynical about everything – I can't really help it. I don't listen to much rock and roll music at all. Yeah, and I don't consider myself a musician, if you can understand that. I'm a workman and that's how I approach my task. I don't think that the Stones are inferior music at all. I think what they do is fine as anything else going around and they deserve the labels as much as the rest, and I'm not resigned to my position like a frustrated jazz musician or anything. This is what I do. Period. And I don't consider myself anything else. *Charlie Watts.*

I'm just into concentrating on what I'm playing and trying to get something together with the people round me ya know? They throw me notes and flowers and things but no one notices. They think I'm just standing there like some sort of dummy. I use up just as much mental energy as anyone but no one appreciates it, [in tone of mock injury].

When we come offstage everyone feels my brow and says "Not a bloody drop" and they're all dripping wet, shirts clinging to them and there's me, all cool and dry, [smiles, amused by it all]. I just don't sweat much. *Bill Wyman.*

They [the public] should expect a lot, because the band has done some really good things, and they should expect a very high standard. I don't feel pressured by it.

They say people expect too much of Paul McCartney, but that's all bollocks. You've got to deliver.

They should expect a high standard from various established bands. I don't think we've fallen a lot below it.

I don't really think about singles any more. I think more expansively. My main hang up is trying to find something to make a whole album exceptional. *Mick Jagger.*

On The Road.

Is there such a thing as a normal person? What's a normal person? I think I'm normal. But most people think I'm not. I don't like to mix with sycophants, but most bands do. They want to hear people tell them how great they are. It's a constant massaging of the ego. But everybody needs that, at least for a few minutes a day. It keeps you sane. *Mick Jagger, 1977.*

Of course I do occasionally arouse primeval instincts, but I mean, most men can do that. They can't do it to so many. I just happen to be able to do it to several thousand people. It's fun to do that. It's really just a game, isn't it? I mean these girls do it to themselves. They're all charged up. It's a dialogue of energy. They give you a lot of energy and take a lot away. Maybe they want something from life, from me. Maybe they think I can give it to them. I don't know.

I get a strange feeling on stage. I feel all the energy coming from the audience.

I feel quite violent sometimes. I quite often want to smash up the microphone or something.

I don't feel the same person on stage as I am normally. *Mick Jagger, 1970.*

41

I don't really look back that much. I haven't thought about it. I don't think I tried necessarily to be outrageous. I move on stage the way I do because I enjoy it. Nothing I do on stage is rehearsed. I don't pose in front of a mirror for hours trying to get it right.

I like it on the road, I don't know what I'd do if I couldn't go out there. I think I'd go mad. It's great to hang around, smash up a few hotel rooms, get drunk. *Mick Jagger.*

There ain't a band in the world that can survive without going on the road. If a band doesn't play in front of people and turn them on at least as much as we do, and I don't think we do it enough, then they're not a band. We should play more regularly. You rehearse for a month, get the tour going, crank it up, and just as you're hitting top gear the last gig comes and it drops for nine months. *Keith Richards,* 1976.

Live Shows.

Yes, I like entertaining . . . I suppose performing is an aid. It helps me as a person, an individual, to get rid of my ego. It's a better process than others. If I get rid of the ego on stage, then the problem ceases to exist when I have left there.

I no longer have a need to prove myself continually to myself. *Mick Jagger,* 1975.

My ego comes across quite nicely on the telly, don't you think? *Mick Jagger,* 1975.

Come to think of it, maybe the reason why the Stones are still going is because we've always been sufficiently aware of what's going on to be influenced, but not so that we slavishly follow trends. *Mick Jagger,* 1974.

The last time I saw you perform in New York, in 1975, you and the group seemed to be involved in fancy stage spectacle, buffoonery and horseplay.

It may have looked like that, but I didn't feel like that. Which means I wasn't acting it properly.

Maybe young kids who had never seen you before thought differently from me.

Exactly, it's easy to say: "Ah, they're not as good as they were before." It may be your eyes that are jaded, rather than *us.*

I saw you performing in 1965, and it was pretty basic then.

The only people who did things like that in the old days were us – a little bit – The Who and the MC5. Everyone else stood up there like a bunch of assholes – they were *terrible*. . . with their suits and ties. The Jam is sort of like an English rock group of 1965, but not as good. You can't really return to basics in big gigs.

You often convey a feeling that combines the fearlessness and rambunctiousness that young kids have, and it seems to be a feeling that charms and bothers people.

It bothers them because they can't be like that themselves. I consider myself very lucky, and one of the reasons for that is that when I'm singing or acting or playing or anything – even at home – I feel just like a baby – like I'm ten or eleven or twelve. Whether that's my fantasy, whether it's right or wrong – I know that it's something that other people can't do. I mean, I can act like a thirty-four-year-old, too – I've trained myself to act in this manner [laughing] – but when I'm playing I can go back in time. I think that's true of many musicians and actors and dancers, and people envy that.

It must be amazing to you that there are all these kids who were three years' old in 1964-1965 and who are seeing you now for the first time.

Sure. I was already in Los Angeles in my pink Cadillac, they were just three years old, and now I go *out* with them [laughing]. It feels all right.

Do you like older women?

No.

And not lying, cheating, vain, affected girls.

It's easy for me to write that kind of song because my talent seems to lie in that direction, and I can only occasionally come up with a really good love song – it's easier to come out with the other side of the coin. So I choose what I do best, that's all. *Mick Jagger,* 1978.

I absolutely draw the line at elephants, man. Even with trousers on. I am not working with animals. It's not in the bleeding contract and it's not gonna be in the gig either. Go on stage with a bloody elephant. Are you mad? I've paid me dues and I'm not working with no animal act. I worked with Elton and that's enough! *Keith Richards,* 1975.

I've seen rock bands just do the same thing every night where it gets like a

HYDE PARK, 1969

43

ON THE ROAD, 1965

The Beatles? I think it's impossible for them to do a tour. Mick has said it before, but it's worth repeating... the Beatles are primarily a recording group. Even though they drew the biggest crowds of their era in North America, I think the Beatles had passed their performing peak even before they were famous. They are a recording band, while our scene is the concerts and many of our records were roughly made on purpose. Our sort of scene is to have a really good time with the audience.

It's always been the Stones' thing to get up on stage and kick the crap out of everything. We had three years of that before we made it, and we were only just getting it together when we became famous. We still had plenty to do on stage, and I think we still have. That's why the tour should be such a groove for us. *Keith Richards,* 1969.

nightclub act. But I don't behave in the same way every night. Spontaneity isn't hard. If I want to jump on the piano I jump on the piano. If I want to go on the floor I go on the floor. If I don't want to go on the floor I don't. There's only so much you can do.

We're no nightclub act. It's not the same every night. People say that a lot and maybe they're right. I've got my doubts whether those people actually saw us. People say self parody of what they were ten years ago. I doubt whether they actually saw us ten years ago. *Mick Jagger,* 1976.

I suppose we could take an elephant on stage and break that up. Really the Who began all this smashing scene and they are the only group I like to see do it. With the others it's just a case of finding bigger things to smash — someone will take a bus on stage soon and smash that up.

I went to one of those "smashing happenings" at the London Roundhouse a few weeks back. I thought everyone would be freaking out and wearing weird clothes but they were all wandering around in dirty macs — it was the most boring thing I've ever seen. Paul McCartney thought everyone would be wearing weird clothes and he went as an Arab, which must have been very lonely for him, because when I went there wasn't another Arab in sight. *Mick Jagger,* 1967.

Did you develop a stage act?
Not really. Mick did his thing and I tried to keep the band together. That's always what it's been, basically. If I'm leapin' about, it's only because something's goin' drastically wrong or it's going drastically right. *Keith Richards.*

I thought the Beatles were awfully nice on telly the other night – didn't you, Keith? John's hair was lovely and fluffy. But they weren't live! I mean were they? I noticed the picture sliding at the beginning of their clip and that's something that only happens on video tape. So I "sussed" it, not that it matters. But they haven't been "live" for years, then, have they? We, on the other hand, never stopped actually doin' it, Top of the Whatsits and all that. Even when they were "live" they weren't

ON THE ROAD, 1975

that *lively* were they? On the other hand we've always been *performers,* y'know? I mean except for a couple of years there. I'd like to do small clubs again and I know I've said that so many times that I feel a bit of a sham now because what we're *actually* doing is three nights at Wembley Pool. It's total hypocrisy – it's like saying "yeah, I'm just the same and I want to do all the same things I did in 1964, but what I'm actually going to do is dress up in a shiny suit and get up in front of 150,000 people. . ."

Concerts are slightly limiting because you feel responsible – you can't just loon off into some insane things: "Hang on five minutes while I try something". . . whereas people in a club don't mind that – they just drink. At a concert you feel like they've got to get their two quids' worth, and you can't stop for long and you've got to jump around in the right place. *Mick Jagger, 1973.*

If people want to listen and they are all sitting there quietly I'll concentrate on playing and give them something for their ears. But if they're screaming I'll forget about solos and just hit it. An artist feeds off an audience and vice versa. Also I think that one of the reasons people go to these shows is to lose a bit of energy. *Keith Richards.*

Stage Fright.

Y'know, like just before we're going onstage, right, and everyone's a bit nervous but we're all too busy tuning up and having a good drink and generally. . . uh, fortifying ourselves. But those guys like Bowie and Lou Reed – you should see 'em, they're petrified. Like everyone is standing around shaking and being totally paranoid. There's no sense of. . . jollity [laughs]. It's like watching slow torture. You've never seen anything like it. *Mick Jagger.*

Hyde Park? Yeah, I can't stop dreaming about it. It had to be the biggest crowd I've ever seen. They were the stars of the show, like some massive religious gathering on the shores of the Ganges. I was a bit shaky at first but then I started

BACKSTAGE AT ALTAMONT, 1969

enjoying myself. *Mick Jagger, 1969.*

I only ever had the butterflies once and that was at the Ealing Club before I went on with Alexis Korner. I was so frightened I had to go out and have half a pint of beer to steady me down.

I've seen performers that were really scared. Once we did an Ed Sullivan show with Jack Jones and he was a bundle of nerves. I mean Ed Sullivan is *nothing* just nothing, but we were all saying "don't worry, it'll be OK." It was probably because we were there.

I think I was nervous at Hyde Park probably, but you just get to such a pitch you can overcome everything. People expect so much of us. They've seen you do it once and think you can do it again. And they can sit back and expect too much; you can't be expected to come on and act daft if they're sitting there like a Sunday school outing, because you just pick it up from them and act staid.

And if it's daytime it's worse because you can see faces and expressions. At least at night you just have the lights and occasional flashes to get off on.
Mick Jagger.

Backup Man.

What do you think gives the Stones their characteristic sound? Why does no other band sound quite like them?

That's something I've tried to analyse with a lot of people. We have a very tight sound for a band that swings, but in amongst that tight sound, it's very ragged as well. Leon Russell and I finally came up with a theory that goes something like this: Every rock 'n' roll band follows the drummer, right? If the drummer slows down, the band slows down with him or speeds up when he does. That's just the way it works – except for our band. Our band does not follow the drummer; our drummer follows the rhythm guitarist, who is Keith Richards.

And that makes the difference?

Yes. Immediately you've got something like a 1/100th of a second delay between the guitar and Charlie's lovely drumming. Now, I'm not putting Charlie down in any way for doing this, but onstage you have to follow Keith. You have no way of *not* following him. You know there's no rigorous twelve bars and then we break and do that bit and then we

come in with four more bars and then Mick does his part – it doesn't work like that. The tune is basically worked out, but it changes all the time; it's very loose. So with Charlie following Keith, you have that very minute delay. Add to that the fact that I've always been able to pick up chord structures very quickly, so I tend to anticipate a bit because I kind of know what Keith's going to do. We've been playing together for so long that I know without even thinking about it. That's why I might be standing there looking at the ceiling when everybody else is looking at Keith to see when the final thing is coming down. I mean, we all make mistakes but basically, I don't need to watch Keith as the other guys tend to do, because I can feel when it's coming. So I tend to anticipate the change, and that puts me that split second ahead of Keith.

What's the result?

When you actually hear that, it seems to just pulse. You know it's right because we're all making stops and starts and it is in time – but it *isn't* as well. That's what we think is the reason for our sound, apart from our style. Everyone thinks, "Oh, Rolling Stones" as soon as they hear one of our fast tunes. And yet sometimes the whole thing can reverse. Charlie will begin to anticipate, and I'll fall behind, but the net result is that loose type of pulse that goes between Keith, Charlie, and me.

How did that begin to happen? Was it a conscious decision or just a matter of personality?

Probably a matter of personality. Keith is a very confident and stubborn player, so he usually thinks someone else has made a mistake. Maybe you'll play halfway through a solo and find that Keith has turned the time around. He'll drop a half- or quarter-bar somewhere, and suddenly Charlie's playing on the beat, instead of on the backbeat – and Keith will not change back – he will doggedly continue until the band changes to adapt to him. It doesn't piss us off in any way, because we all expect it to happen. He knows in general that we're following him, so he doesn't care if he changes the beat around or isn't really aware of it. He's quite amusing like that. Sometimes Keith will be playing along, and suddenly he becomes aware that Charlie's playing on the beat, and he'll turn around and point like, "Aha, gotcha!"

Like Charlie made the mistake?

Yeah, and Charlie will be so surprised

and suddenly realise he's on the beat for some reason, and he hasn't changed at all. And then he'll be very uptight to get back in, because it's very hard for a drummer to swap the beat. So it's a mite funny sometimes, but it does happen, especially on the intros. Some of the intros are quite samey sounding. I mean, if you're doing a riff on one chord with the inflections that Keith uses, and you're not hearing too well with the screaming crowds, you cannot tell if you are coming in on or off the beat. 'Street Fighting Man' [the live version is on *Get Yer Ya-Yas Out*] is a tune that this tends to happen on.

Doesn't Charlie have monitor speakers?

Well, he's got monitors, but in those circumstances it's very difficult to hear the accents – the difference between the soft and hard strokes. The problem is that he's often totally unaware that he's on the wrong beat, and he shuts his eyes and pulls his mouth up, you know, and he's gone. You can't even catch his eye because they're closed. Someone has to go up and kick the cymbal. I don't think that happens too often with other bands; I don't hear those very simple kinds of mistakes going on with other bands. But I think that's a little of the charm of the Stones. They're not infallible, and we know that. Everybody else might as well know it, too.

Why do you think it works so well?

I don't know, but our band has always seemed to function very well against the rules. None of us are superb musicians in a technical or performing sense. It's just that we have that mixture within the band, and Ron Wood has really dropped into that. Mick Taylor didn't, really. He's very technical and a very clever musician – much more clever musically than the rest of us, I think. That's probably why he didn't jell with us as well as Woody does. Woody's a very good musician, of course, but much more 'Stonesy,' if you like, more like Keith's playing than pretty. *Bill Wyman, 1978.*

White drummers don't swing, except for Charlie Watts. *Keith Richards, 1977.*

It's not that it's easy working with the same drummer, it's just so *natural*. If he makes a mistake I just naturally follow. But then that applies to the whole band. Keith can change a beat half way through or drop a bar. Charlie does it as well but you just

click in half a second and you're back into it.

You learn to think alike so if a situation arises, like Charlie breaking a stick, you all do the same thing. It comes naturally, not by talking about it, or working out what you're gonna do, it just *happens*. I know what Keith will do if something happens, Charlie knows. It's so natural you just do it. *Bill Wyman.*

I just lay back and fatten the sound. *Bill Wyman, 1974.*

The Survivors.

How come you pick on him [Ron Wood] so much?

Wellllll, he picks on me, you know... We're just doing this sort of David [Bowie] and Mick Ronson routine. *Mick Jagger, 1975.*

How do you like it, Ron?

I think Mick's been dying to get his hands on another guitarist. He came up to me and said, "If I come and attack you... you don't mind do you?" He really loves to make it look real.

In Montauk, when we were rehearsing, we'd be sitting there playing and he'd suddenly come up and kick me. And he tried it on Charlie's drums – once. He never tried it again. Charlie did a mild flip-out, said, "Listen, I don't unplug your mike lead, so don't upset my drums. And while we're at it, don't keep buggin' Ronnie." *Ron Wood, 1975.*

And there's such a great rapport going now between the band that people actually say to each other, "You played great tonight!" – which we'd never say. That's never been said in twelve years. I've never been told, *ever*, "You did a great set tonight." I've only been told, "You were out of tune tonight." If I play great, it's accepted, and it's the same with Charlie. If you play badly or something goes wrong, you get put down, so you never get that uplift, but Woody started to get that happening, and now everybody congratulates everybody, and it's "Thanks for a great show!" We were all bumping into each other after the last show of the tour and everybody was saying to everybody else individually, "Thanks for a great tour, man," *thanking* each other for how good the tour was, and

RON WOOD, 1975/ANNIE LIEBOWITZ (COLORIFIC)

THE FRONT ROW 1975/ANNIE LIEBOWITZ

we'd never do that before. And I really got off on that. Woody's fabulous! He's made this band come back to life again!
Bill Wyman, 1978.

Back In The Clubs.

Why do you find it more relaxing to play a small club, than, say, a stadium?

Well, you can *talk* to the people. If you've busted a string, you say, "Look darlin', hold on, I've busted a bleedin' string and I've gotta fix it." Whereas, when you're forty feet away from the first row, you're conscious of that gap before you're conscious of the audience.

It's ironic that you're more comfortable in a place where you're closely watched. I mean, they can see if your fly's unzipped. . .

Right. But once you're at that level, they can see that you're the same as them so you get all that bullshit out of the way.

At a concert hall, with people seated so high up it's like they're floating down from heaven, it's almost as if they're watching a movie except they can't see as good.

In a small place you're face to face with them. They can see how many spots you've got and how many teeth are left and whether your eyeballs are pinned. That's all over in the first few minutes so then it's just a matter of them enjoying themselves. *Keith Richards,* 1977.

I mean we haven't played in a place that small [El Mocambo Club, Toronto] since '62. But it was dead easy to get back into. It all fell into place, it felt very natural, you know. It's been a long time since I've had my legs stroked while playing, you know. I've forgotten about that . . . it's a full circle. Mind you the first night the band sounds like it was playing for something in New Delhi; there were all these weird sort of quarter tones, out of tune, very frantic; it was all the adrenalin. *Keith Richards,* 1977.

Drugs.

The general public even *now* doesn't know what really happens and what people are really like, y'know what I mean? Like people in Japan think I'm walking around with needles stuck up me arms, y'know? They *do*, they seriously believe it. I mean they think I'm incoherent, idiotic, y'know, junkie. To me, I'm just an ordinary English bloke, same as everyone else. And so are most English musicians. And you know that. Some of them are a bit loony but they're perfectly straight-up people, y'know, mostly workin' class and that. And when it comes to dealin' with taxi drivers and that or bus conductors, I mean, they're the same, y'know. But you gotta put it down to one of those ridiculous things that happen *Mick Jagger,* 1974.

A lot of kids don't want to live the same sort of lives as their parents and their parents don't recognise their right to choose a different life because they are so conditioned. But things are going to change because it's now like two forces, with youth on one side, and both are getting bigger and stronger.

    I don't like the way police attitudes have changed. They're getting new power and it's growing at an alarming rate because once something is that big it wants to get bigger. It is becoming a social police, more and more concerned with how you live. *Keith Richards,* 1967.

Regretfully I never took acid. I say regretfully because I've been terrified of the fucking stuff and I wish I'd taken it to know about it. I think I was the only rock star never to wear a pair of beads. I wished I could have done, but it never looked right on me. But I thought it was great. It fucked a lot of people up, the psychedelic thing, but it made people really talk to each other, too.

    People say I've always been Charlie. I don't know. Maybe I'd have been a better person if I had gone through all that. Like junk. I don't like it. I've never had it. I don't want it. I can hear better behind a smoke but I can cope with that. But I

drink, too, and I can't cope with that sometimes.

    Part of it is that I never was a teenager, man. I'd be off in the corner talking about Kierkegaard. I always took myself seriously and thought Buddy Holly was a great joke. *Charlie Watts.*

I don't think 'Sticky Fingers' is a heavy drug album any more than the world is a heavy world. In 1964, I didn't use to run into cats in America who'd come up to me and say, "Do you want some skag? Do you want some coke? Do you want some acid? Do you want some peyote?" And then go through all those initials and names. Now you have trouble avoiding them.

    People who think you're ready to finance every drug smuggling expedition in the world. "Hey listen, I'm not interested. You got the wrong idea". The cats that are into it are into it because they're good at . . . they've taken their chances at it. They're not doing it for nothing, it's either they're getting their rocks off or they're into it for bread. A lot of cats get their kicks going through customs. So what, man? *Keith Richards.*

What I think about drugs. Firstly, I don't think anyone should go to prison for drugs unless, like, they're makin' millions out of it, y'know, and just like makin' people's lives a misery. I don't think people who take drugs should be put away in prisons. I don't think that's gonna have any effect on them whatsoever. I don't think people should be stopped from movin' from A to B merely because they've been convicted on some minor charge. I also don't think hard drugs are very good for anyone because I don't think most people can handle them. I mean, y'know, you don't have to be a musician to know that. You just have to come to America. Or you just have to stand in Piccadilly Circus. I don't think that people can handle drugs period. People can't. A lot of people can't handle alcohol. A lot of people can't handle anything, y'know. A lot of people are

"NUDE GIRL AT STONES PARTY", 1967/MICHAEL COOPER

addicted to hard drugs, they just can't handle them. They get ill, they rely on them, y'know, fall to bits, y'know. I mean it's 'orrible, that's what I think about them. *Mick Jagger, 1974.*

I think the way they treated Brian was terrible — you know, mentioning drugs the first thing — but that was mainly the Sundays. *Keith Richards.*

Law And Disorder.

When the prosecuting counsel asked me about chicks in nothing but fur rugs I said, "I'm not concerned with your pretty morals, which are illegitimate." They couldn't take that one. *Keith Richards.*

The *News of the World* got hold of someone who was working for us. I think it was the cat who was driving me at the time. They knew we were going to be down there at a party. Really, just something I'd done a million times before and I've done a million times since. I simply said, "Let's go down to my place for a weekend." It just so happened we all took acid and were in a completely freaked out state when they arrived. They weren't ready for that.

There's a big knock at the door. Eight o'clock. Everybody is just sort of gliding down slowly from the whole day of sort of freaking about. Everyone has

managed to find their way back to the house. TV is on with the sound off and the record player is on. Strobe lights are flickering. Marianne Faithfull has just decided that she wanted a bath and has wrapped herself up in a rug and is watching the box.

'Bang, bang, bang', this big knock at the door and I go to answer it. "Oh look, there's lots of little ladies and gentlemen outside." He says, "Read this," and I'm going "Wha', wha'? All right".

There was this other pusher there who I really didn't know. He'd come with some other people and was sitting there with a big bag of stash. They even let him go, out of the country. He wasn't what they were looking for.

When it came down to it, they couldn't pin anything at all on us. All they could pin on me was allowing people to smoke on my premises. It wasn't my shit. All they could pin on Mick was these four amphetamine tablets that he'd bought in Italy across the counter. It really backfired on them because they didn't get enough on us. They had more on the people who were with us who they weren't interested in. There were lots of people there they didn't even bring up on charges. *Keith Richards.*

BRIAN JONES AND PRINCE STANISLAS KLOSSOWSKI DE ROWLA
LEAVE COURT CHARGED WITH POSSESSION OF CANNABIS, 1967/POPPERFOTO

We were just gliding off from a twelve hour trip. You know how that freaks people out when they walk in on you. The vibes were so funny for them. I told one of the women with them they'd brought to search the ladies, "Would you mind stepping off that Moroccan cushion? Because you're ruining the tapestries." We were playing it like that. They tried to get us to turn the record player off and we said, "No. We won't turn it off but we'll turn it down." As they went, as they started going out the door, somebody put on 'Rainy Day Women' really loud. Everybody must get stoned. And that was it.

What usually happens is that someone gets busted, the papers have it the next day. For a week they held it back to see how much bread they could get off us. Nothing was said for a week. They wanted to see. Unfortunately none of us knew what to do, who to bum the bread to and so went via slightly the wrong people and it didn't get up all the way.

Mick can tell you how much. It was his bread. Quite a bit of bread.

Eventually after a couple of weeks

the papers said the Rolling Stones have been raided for possession. The first court thing didn't come up for three months. Just a straight hearing. That was cool. The heavy trial came in June, about five months after. It was really starting to wear us out by then. The lawyers were saying, "It seems really weird, they want to really do it to you."

The harassment took its toll on Brian, it really did. Y'see what I mean? The second time, the blow was just too much, he couldn't take it. He was just too sensitive, y'know. Some people might say too weak but I mean he wasn't a criminal. Here was a guy, he was just a fuckin' musician man, you know – you've got to be tough to be a criminal. If you choose to be a criminal, you've got to rob people, pick pockets, you gotta be tough like, take what's coming to you and all that. This guy's a musician and he just wants to get on playing his music and he's just been harassed *all the time* and he just can't take it. And that's it, man. *Mick Jagger,* 1974.

It didn't hit me for months because I

hadn't seen him a lot. The only time we'd see him was down at the courthouse, at one of his trials. They really roughed him up, man. He wasn't the cat that could stand that kind of shit and they really went for him like when hound dogs smell blood. "There's one that'll break if we keep on." And they busted him and busted him. That cat got so paranoid at the end like they did to Lenny Bruce, the same tactics. Break him down. Maybe with Mick and me they felt, well they're old lads. *Keith Richards,* 1971.

It was a painful year, y'know. '67 was a year of change for everybody. I guess '67 was the explosion of the drug culture if there is such a thing, it came into the open from underground y'know and everybody started talking about it. And through this whole year we were having to put up with this incredible hassle, this sort of continual confrontation with policemen and judges. I really feel very uncomfortable looking at a uniform anyway and having to deal with those people for a whole year. It did wear us down a bit. In fact, it put us on our back, really, for eighteen months or so. It wasn't until we got into 'Beggars Banquet' that the whole thing vanished into the past. But at the time they were still bugging Brian like mad. And Mick. The police probably were going into thousands of homes in England every day with a warrant. That's the law, they're allowed to do it and that's the way it is y'know? There were certain aspects of that case, a few that went on behind the scenes which are very unsavoury and which once and for all destroyed for me faith and fairness, impartiality of the English judicial system. Except when you've really created a fuss and got it up to the highest then they start reconsidering, but I found out what they were like, y'know, and for that I'm grateful because I hate to be labouring under delusions. At least I know that English cops are no better or no worse than anywhere else, y'know. I just wish they wouldn't pretend they're something that they're not. *Keith Richards,* 1974.

I don't know what I feel about the busts. It's very difficult to put into perspective because I'm still being harassed. They were really nasty and mean. I mean all that handcuffs, on four pep pill charges. It's just daft. The more I think about it – I hardly ever do – but it was just so absurd,

they tried to blow it up into a whole thing that was like. . . that's the way the establishment works, particularly the police, y'know. I'm not saying the judges, but the police were like. . . they like to make it more than it ever is and is ever gonna be. They don't think they've got anything going unless they've got the kitchen thrown in. Oh God. *Mick Jagger,* 1974.

Jail Bait.

I think I came quite close [to jail]. Brian really came close to doing six months and a friend actually did six months. I think it was all so disgraceful and very stupid and so English. *Mick Jagger.*

I was sittin' in jail and some one throws it [*The Times*] through the window, which is illegal in jail. Very nice, I mean it was what got me out and helped get us off I think because it was against the normal press conduct and shows a strong sense of purpose. That was something I'll always remember and be grateful for. *Mick Jagger,* 1974.

How did you feel about being imprisoned in Lewes jail?
It was disgraceful. Disgraceful. I didn't feel alone while I was in there because I knew that a lot of people disagreed with how we were being treated, but on the other hand I felt that people were just using us. Now if you do that kind of thing to some people it makes them strong and if you do it to others it can quickly destroy them and it destroyed Brian, which was very sad.
He just couldn't take it. *Mick Jagger.*

It took the cops a full half hour to wake me up. It's pretty frightening waking up with cops all round your bed. *Keith Richards,* 1977.

It was about four or five days. That was enough. Enough to put me off wanting to go, I can tell you. It was horrible. It was really weird. A strange existence. You just don't want to get involved if you can avoid it. I remember asking the guy if I could go out for exercise, because it was the exercise period. And the guy said, "You don't want to go out there with all those criminals, do you?"

I had to get a job, because in prison everyone had a job. I was going to be put down for a librarian, but I never did get to see what the scope was. Before you are convicted they treat you differently. You can keep your own clothes and everything. Then you have to wear the prison clothes. I wasn't there long enough for that.

A guy threw a newspaper into my cell. It was *The Times* with an editorial piece on me. I got out by the afternoon. Of course I didn't want to go back, but I've been in prison since, in Rhode Island, near Boston. I was in prison there in 1975 for a little while. Got arrested for trying to stop Keith being arrested. Obstructing the course of justice. I think I said, "Here, don't do that, we've got a concert to do." "Okay, you too." Keith had hit somebody and was arrested. It was probably a journalist, like you. Oh, it was too awful. But nothing happened in the case. *Mick Jagger, 1977.*

Wormwood Scrubs is a hundred and fifty years old, man. I wouldn't even want to play there, much less live there. They take me inside. They don't give you a knife and fork, they give you a spoon with very blunt edges so you can't do yourself in. They don't give you a belt, in case you hang yourself. It's that bad in there.

They give you a little piece of paper and a pencil. Both Robert and I, the first thing we did is sit down and write. "Dear Mum, don't worry . . . I'm in here and someone's working to get me out, da-da-da." Then you're given your cell. And they start knocking on the bars at six in the morning to wake you up.

All the other prisoners started dropping bits of tobacco through for me, because in any jail tobacco is the currency. Some of them were really great. Some of them were in for life. Shoving papers under the door to roll it up with. The first thing you do automatically when you wake up is drag the chair to the window and look up to see what you can see out the window. It's an automatic reaction. That one little square of sky, trying to reach it.

It's amazing. I was going to have to make those little Christmas trees that go on cakes. And sewing up mailbags. Then there's the hour walk when you have to keep moving round in a courtyard. Cats coming up behind me, it's amazing, they can talk without moving their mouths. "Want some hash? Take acid? In here?"

Most of the prisoners were really great. "What you doing in here? Bastards. They just wanted to get you." They filled me in. "They've been waiting for you in here for ages," they said. So I said, "I ain't going to be in here very long, baby, don't worry about that."

And that afternoon, they had the radio playing, this fucking Stones record comes on. And the whole prison started, "Rayyyyy!" Going like mad. Banging on the bars. They knew I was in and they wanted to let me know.

They took all the new prisoners to have their photographs taken sitting on a swivel stool, looked like an execution chamber. Really hard. Face and profile. Those are the sort of things they'll do automatically if they pick you up in America, you get fingerdabs and photographs. In England, it's a much heavier scene. You don't get photographed and fingerprinted until you've been convicted.

Then they take you to the padre and the chapel and the library, you're allowed one book and they show you where you're going to work and that's it. That afternoon, I'm lying in my cell wondering what the fuck was going on and suddenly someone yelled, "You're out, man, you're out. It's just been on the news." So I started kicking the shit out of the door. I said, "You let me out, you bastards, I got bail."

So they took me to the governor's office and signed me out. And when it got up to the appeal court, they just threw it out in ten minutes. This judge had just blown it. I mean, he said things to me while I was up there that if I'd caught him by himself I'd have wrung his neck. When he gave me the year sentence, he called me "scum" and "filth" and "People like this shouldn't be . . . " *Keith Richards.*

I Got Nasty Habits.

If you're going to get into junk, it stands to reason you should . . . for a start, in guys particularly, it takes the place of everything. You don't need a chick, you don't need music, you don't need nothing. It doesn't get you anywhere. It's not called junk for nothing. Why did Burroughs kick it, after twenty five years?

MICK JAGGER 1967/POPPERFOTO

People have offered me a lot of things over the years, mainly to keep going. "Work, you bastard. Take one of these." I've tried a lot of shit. I don't even know what it is. I personally think . . . it depends if you're ready. Same with alcohol. You should find out what it does. If you don't know what it does and you're just putting it in, for the sake of it, you're a dummy.

What it does depends on what form you take it in. Some people snort, some people shoot it. You tell me what it does. The Peruvians, they chew it, and that's the trip. You can buy it in any grocery store and you eat it with a hunk of lime-stone and it just freezes you. At 11,000 feet it's hard to breathe anyway. Those cats have 47 per cent more red corpuscles than us lowlanders. Huge lungs, and they're chewing it all the time. You buy it along with your eggs and your lemons. It depends how you take it.
Keith Richards, 1973.

I once took that apomorphine cure that Burroughs swears by. Dr. Dent was dead, but his assistant whom he trained, this lovely old dear called Smitty, who's like mother hen, still runs the clinic. I had her down to my place for five days, and she just sort of comes in and says, "Here's your shot, dear, there's a good boy," or, "You've been a naughty boy, you've taken something, yes you have, I can tell".

But it's a pretty medieval cure. You just vomit all the time. *Keith Richards.*

Electro-acupuncture . . . it's so simple it's not true. But as to whether or not they'll ever let people know about it is another thing. I can't tell you how it works

because they don't even know for sure. All they know is that it does work. It's a little metal box with leads that clip on to your ears, and in two or three days . . . which is the worst period for kicking junk . . . in those 72 hours it leaves your system.

Actually, you should be incredibly sick, but for some reason you're not. Why? I don't know, because all it is is a very simple electronic nine volt battery-run operation. *Keith Richards, 1978.*

What effect did acid have on your personality?

[Laughs] It drove me completely insane. No – I'm joking.

You know what I mean, some took the trip like Eric Burdon and. . .

. . . And never came back. We came back in 1968. It didn't give me permanent brain-damage or anything at all like that. I shouldn't really own up to it even now. I took it before it was made illegal. . . well, isn't that what people used to say?

Actually, speaking of Burdon, the last time I saw him he kept yelling "Beer and Acid" at me, which was very peculiar, but then, I was very peculiar at the time as well. However, I quite enjoyed it. . . I thought it was lovely. *Mick Jagger, 1974.*

Do you regret starting to take hard drugs?

No, I don't regret nuthin'. I just got bored with it. It would take more than the Mounties to turn me off something. If I really wanted to stay on it, I'd stay on it. Because I know damn well that in prison you can get as much as you want. When I was in prison in England in 1967 my first day there, another inmate tapped me on the shoulder and asked me if I wanted some hash. That was years ago. Can you imagine what it must be like now? All you've gotta do is bend over twice or have the right amount of tobacco and you've got whatever you want.

But do you feel better mentally now you've given up heroin?

Different and I suppose you could say healthier. Although I must say in fairness to the poppy that never once did I have a cold. The cure for the common cold is there, but they daren't tell anybody because they would have a nation full of dope addicts. I don't recommend drugs to anybody. It's really wrong when twelve year olds are on the streets scoring dope with strychnine thrown in to give it an extra flash. The worst thing is the ignorance of people taking things without knowing what they're doing.

You need the freedom and life style to be able to indulge in drugs.

I don't know if it's that. Half the reason I got drawn into it was because I didn't have a lot of freedom and time off. If I'd had the freedom I could have dragged myself off to somewhere remote for three months and cleaned myself up and pulled myself together. But in this business there is always a new tour to do, and before you know it, five years have gone. I started getting hooked ten years ago. That was into squeezing blackheads! Now I'm pulling out grey hairs – ha ha!

But now I can remember what each show was like afterwards, without having somebody tell me. I did a lot of shows when I was completely out of my brain. One show was just like another, and it was like a tunnel that got smaller and smaller. *Keith Richards.*

I was on and off junk for ten years. But – and I want to make this clear – that doesn't prescribe it for anybody else. *Keith Richards, 1978.*

Originally that was just an overall observation. I went through it and didn't feel anything in particular. . . I don't know, though. I was thirty-three last year and the effect has taken a few months to make itself felt. There was that whole Toronto incident and at the end of that I just knew I had to finish with dope. So I guess I did undergo something of a traumatic experience at thirty-three. . . *Keith Richards, 1978.*

You could be sick as a dog but as long as you've got a suntan, everybody thinks you're in great shape. *Keith Richards, 1977.*

Blood On The Tracks.

There's no denying that there's a high fatality rate in rock and roll. Up until the middle sixties the most obvious method of rock and roll death was chartered planes. Since then drugs have taken their toll, but all the people that I've known that have died from so-called drug over-doses have all been people that've had some fairly serious physical weakness somewhere.

I think that, personally, it's purely a matter of the person concerned. I mean, it's like a good blowjob. You know, in some States that's still illegal. It's just a matter of how far people are prepared to put up with so-called authorities prying into their lives. If they really don't want to accept it, then they'll do something about it, because there'll be no way they can enforce it. *Keith Richards.*

Before I even knew what drugs were everybody had believed we were out of our heads. They'd come up to us in Richmond and Ealing with that sidelong look that people had in those days, when it was very taboo and mysterioso exotic, and they'd whisper, "What are you on?" And I'd say "Well actually, I just had a brown and mild."

I don't think musicians are necessarily attracted to a drug lifestyle. They just come into contact with it more than most people because. . . look, a cat plays a club, and that's where the local pusher hangs out to supply the kids; the guy naturally gets into contact with the musicians playing there.

That's the only connection I can think of in the first place. There may be a whole culture on the West Coast devoted to drugs but it hasn't sustained anything musically. I don't think drugs have added anything to music, let's put it that way.

They might have flashed the inspiration for a couple of good songs, but I don't think there's anything fantastic been written under the influence of drugs that couldn't have been written without. But you find out what it's like because it's there.

It's like the desire to climb Everest, to attempt it because it challenges the experimental instincts.

But dangerous, too. The newspaper headlines stand out vividly. "Hendrix, Morrison, Joplin – victims of the drug culture."

Because they died, *because they died.* . . Before they weren't seen as that. With Hendrix, people either just dug him or they thought he was some evil, nasty, drug-taking black man, which was the other half of his image to moms and dads across the land. But once you're dead, you're the "victim of the drug culture."

When a rock star dies, it's got a romantic tinge to it, but actually it's very sordid.

It's always sad when somebody really good and obviously still into it suddenly

just. . . [he snaps his fingers abruptly] just like that. I mean, some people do die young and that's all there is to it.

Some people have said it all by the time they're twenty-two or twenty-five, but I don't get that feeling with Hendrix or Janis Joplin. I don't think they were finished, or that it was their time to go. [He casts an ironic eye] They may all have died because they had "J" and "I" in their name, who knows? Brian Jones, Jim Morrison, Janis Joplin, Jimi Hendrix. . . Mick Jagger! *Keith Richards.*

I was reading a history of Big Bill Broonzy nicked from Hendon library the other day, and there was a little bit in there where he said that if he were to put a band together again he'd have pot smokers instead of drinkers. They don't forget their notes and they're on time. *Keith Richards,* 1977.

Victimisation.

I see these phony workmen outside my front door every day; I'm moving very shortly. *Keith Richards.*

The trouble with recording is that you're standing still and you attract the attention of the police and everybody else. It's much better to be on the move. They're [the police] rather slow thinking, so that before they know you're there you're gone. *Keith Richards,* 1978.

They go through you at the customs and that applies to everyone with you. It's a hassle. I was on bail once when we were on the road and it was a nightmare. I was at the airport for six hours. I was on bail in England and I was going to Switzerland from America, at the end of 1969. I had the trial in 1970. That was for marijuana. *Mick Jagger,* 1977.

I feel very hopeful about the future. I find it all very enjoyable, with a few peak surprises thrown in. Even being busted. . .. it's no pleasure, but it certainly isn't boring. And I think boring is the worst thing of all, you know, anything but boring.

At least it keeps you active. *Keith Richards.*

Why me? Why am I always the bag man? *Keith Richards.*

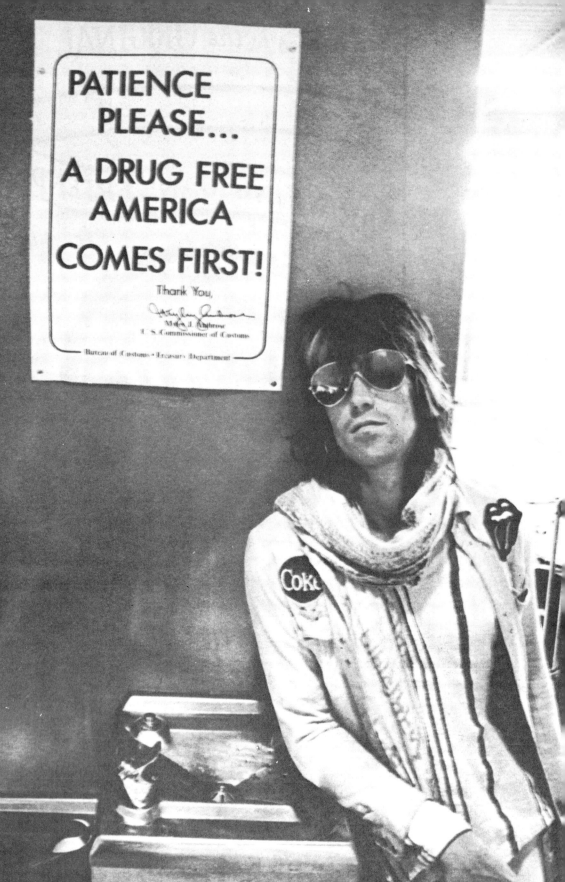

England/U.S.A.

I'm, along with the Queen, y'know – one of the best things England's got – me and the Queen. *Mick Jagger,* 1978.

You actually go down to Kentucky, Louisville, and they've got bourbons that make Old Grandad and Jack Daniels look like Schweppes bitter lemon . . . there's one called, ah, Rebel Yell and that's dynamite shit. *Keith Richards.*

I remember once in Philadelphia some kids had picked up on an interview Brian had done with somebody, he'd used one of those intellectual words like "esoteric". And so, right in the front, these kids had big signs that said, "Brian, you're so esoteric". It had that aura. It was down to *Sixteen* magazine. Everything you did in America then, it could all be in *Sixteen* magazine. *Keith Richards.*

American Dreams.

America was a real fantasy land. It was still Walt Disney and hamburger dates and when you came back in 1969 it wasn't any more. Kids were really into what was going on in their country. I remember watching Goldwater-Johnson in '64 and it was a complete little show. But by the time it came to Nixon's turn two years ago, people were concerned in a really different way. *Keith Richards,* 1969.

On our first expedition to the United States we noticed a distinct lack of crumpet, as we put it in those days. It was very difficult, man. For cats who had done Europe and England, scoring chicks right, left and centre, to come to a country where apparently no one believed in it. We really got down to the lowest and worked our way up again. Because it was difficult.
 In New York or L.A., you can always find something in a city that big if that's what you want. But when you're in Omaha in 1964 and you suddenly feel

horny, you might as well forget it. In three years, in two years, every time you went back it was . . . the next time back it was like, it only took someone from outside to come in and hit the switch somewhere. *Keith Richards,* 1973.

We were very unsuccessful at first but we still liked it. You see, we knew that we just had to make it in America. There we were touring all over the place on our own and nobody seemed to know us. Touring on our own wasn't too bad in a way, but there was this total apathy building up from just about everyone. Everything was all wrong.
 Nobody has ever done it all in one go . . . it takes time to "conquer" America. It took the Beatles two years to break through in the States. *Mick Jagger.*

We did a date in Minneapolis which was organised only two days before. Nobody had heard of us. I think the reaction was the same as we first experienced in England a year ago – complete disbelief and curiosity. There weren't many people there because the tickets were three dollars. *Bill Wyman.*

It was the only TV show we did that time. Dean Martin was so insulting, saying, "Don't leave me backstage with those morons. The smell back there is awful. I can see the fleas jumping off them. Ha ha ha." We did three songs for them and when the thing was shown there was about two and a half minutes of us. We were like a joke act for them. We watched it on tour and got sick. It was our only way of getting across, and after we saw it we said, "That's it. Let's go home then. Let's just pack it in and forget it."
 But then we got lucky and had a couple of good shows in a row and after we'd had some big records in the States, they re-ran that Hollywood Palace show six times, with new MCs saying, "And now the fabulous Rolling Stones", with screams and cheers added in the background. *Bill Wyman.*

When we arrived in the States we didn't have a hit record or anything really going for us, if I remember I think 'Not Fade Away' was about number 82 on the charts the week we arrived. All the other English groups who had ever been to the States had at least a number one or perhaps two number one records to their credit. We had nothing, except that we were English.

We had a really bad tour, then about halfway through it we all wanted to pack up and come home. That was directly after Dean Martin had really fucked us up on that Hollywood Palace TV show . . . that was really bad.

When we finally got back to London we had this great Welcome Back thing which I think was held at the Royal Albert Hall, and the kids were just great. More than anything, that gave us encouragement and things just got better and better after that. So except for that first American tour there has never been any lack of morale within the band.

I don't think that there's ever been a time when we've ever thought of breaking up. The great thing about our band is that we never really fight amongst ourselves. *Bill Wyman, 1965.*

American Nightmares.

It's a lot of rubbish and typically American now, isn't it? It's like the old Mothers' Legion banning Elvis. There are some weird people who stand up on their soapbox and preach that "you are undermining the morals of the young America" and all that sort of crap. I mean, who are they trying to kid, making out that their kids don't know anything about it all and that 'Puff the Magic Dragon' is about drug addiction? Well, if somebody can write a song and get two meanings like that it's pretty clever, but you have to look pretty far to find that second meaning. The bit about "I'm a King Bee" — well, that's one of the great old blues lyrics and they didn't even know that. I think maybe the article could help us. They printed our picture, and you know they always say it doesn't matter what the writer says as long as he spells the name right. *Keith Richards.*

Censorship is still with us in a number of ugly forms. But the days when men like comedian Lenny Bruce and artist Jim Dine are persecuted are coming to an end. Young people are measuring opinion with new yardsticks and it must mean greater individual freedom of expression. Pop music will have its part to play in all this. When certain American folk artists with important messages to tell are no longer suppressed maybe we'll arrive nearer the truth.

The lyrics of 'Satisfaction' were subjected to a form of critical censorship in America. This must go. Lennon's recent piece of free speech was the subject of the same bigoted thinking. But the new generation will do away with all this – I hope. *Brian Jones, 1967*

It was then I realised what Lenny Bruce was talking about. We were sitting back in the dressing room. First time in Omaha in '64. Drinking whisky and coke out of cups, paper cups, just waiting to go on. Cops walked in. "What's that?" "You can't drink whisky in a public place." I happened to be drinking just coke actually. "Tip it down the bog." I said, "No, man, I've just got Coca-Cola in here."

I looked up and I got a .44 looking at me, right between the eyes. Here's a cop, telling me to tip Coca-Cola down the bog. Wouldn't be there if it wasn't for Coca-Cola. But that's when I realised what it could get into. *Keith Richards, 1970.*

Drug Culture.

You know, during World War II the number of junkies in America dropped to almost zero because they just policed the fucking ports properly.

In wartime everything just snaps into action, right? You can't get anything into that country unless they want it in.

Which means they can do it if they want to, if they really wanted to stop it. But you can make more money out of heroin than you can out of anything else. *Keith Richards.*

America has changed, believe me, quite considerably in the last ten years, but it doesn't appear to if you just look at the country.

Take the FBI. It still pokes its nose, but not only does it now have another chief but it's lost the guy who started the whole shebang, who was the FBI.

ON BROADWAY, 1964

Ten years ago America was just a big put-on. It was exactly what every English person thought it to be, except much more so, with dating rings, holding hands, hamburgers and teenage heaven – it was all there! In '63, '64. Ugh! Would you kiss her on your first date? That was the burning question, then. [". . . Only if she's got bad breath," mutters Jagger.] And now? [the crafty look of the dealer,] Oh, it's "want some acid, man, want some acid?" You know. *Keith Richards.*

I wouldn't live in America. I don't like the country enough. I prefer England. The atmosphere is too much for me. Life is too fast here with everyone rushing around like a lot of idiots. I don't like the food because the menus lack variety. The transport cafes are better than the transport cafes in Britain but the good restaurants here are not anywhere near as good. All the food tastes pre-packed. About the only thing I like about their food is their thick ham that I have for breakfast . . . You can't get Russian vodka. They won't import it and so they make their own in Florida. They let anybody in the hotels even if they're not

staying there. So that means that sometimes we get fans knocking on our door at six o'clock in the morning . . . On the whole the Americans are very generous people, but they're very rude. The police are unbelievable. In the south they look like cowboys, wearing stetsons and carrying guns and riding motorbikes. In towns they look like they do on the films. And they're not quietly spoken like they are in Britain. In fact, they're loud mouthed. In Britain I think they're a bit fed up with knocking us. The knockers here are madder than in Britain and more demonstrative. They're just twisted out of their minds. Because they think everything that is ever said about us is serious, lots of people think we're being hit around and are pawns in the hands of publicity men. You've only got to give a joke answer to a question and they make it into a serious statement of fact

we go everywhere by car. Even then in the hotel lobby the other day an eighty year old woman asked me if I was one of the Supremes! She wasn't kidding. *Mick Jagger, 1964.*

The drug culture, has a fantastic grip on American kids. Sociologists ask why.

Is it because America has refused to face up to the problem, like England has, which is just to give people who want smack, smack. Give it to 'em and then it's cool.

In England there hasn't been that enormous increase in junkies, and also they don't go around thieving, stealing and mugging to get bread for their next fix, which is what happens in America.

For a nation that can put a man on the moon it isn't that much of a problem to find a cure for heroin addiction, not if they really wanted to. *Keith Richards.*

Oh, Britain's going down the tubes? Well, they've driven out everyone who was any good. Even those staunch Britishers Reg and Rod, who two years ago swore they would never leave Britain, the minute their mansions were threatened they were in L.A. like a shot. You go to L.A. these days and it's a colony of English rock stars. I don't know why they want to go to L.A. I like to go there for two weeks and get the fuck out. *Mick Jagger.*

Poor Old England.

The English are very strange. They're tolerant up to a point where they're told not to be. You get to a point up there where somebody turns around and swings a little finger. They haven't been fucked since Cromwell man.

First they don't like young kids with a lot of money. But as long as you don't bother them, that's cool. But we bothered them. We bothered 'em because of the way we looked, the way we'd act. Because we never showed any reverence for them whatsoever. Whereas the Beatles had. They'd gone along with it so far, with the MBE's and shaking hands. Whenever we were asked about things like that we'd say, "Fuck it. Don't want to know about things like that. Bollocks. Don't need it." That riled 'em somewhere. *Keith Richards, 1971.*

A knighthood, I'd take, nothing less than a knighthood. But you gotta last a long time to get a knighthood.

Noel Coward was one of the most hated people in England at one point but he got a knighthood. In the *Way of Tao* I think it says no government should ever decorate anyone because it makes other people jealous and I think I agree with that. *Mick Jagger, 1974.*

America? Their way of thinking can be as antiquated as our standard of living. *Keith Richards, 1966.*

They come up to me in the street in Switzerland and say, "Hey, you're a Rolling Stone! I'm in a band. How do we get to be really big and earn lots of money? What do you have to do to make a good group?"

And I say, "Well, look, why don't you try starving?" They can't even comprehend that, man, they're so rich. I mean, have you ever heard of a good Swiss musician, a good Swiss painter or writer?

England gets fooled by the newspapers and TV that if it doesn't have the best standard of living in the world at least it's got the second best. England doesn't even know, man! They're being fooled all along the line.

People in Switzerland, France and Germany live twice as good as anybody in England. They're twice as bourgeois, twice as rich. *Keith Richards.*

The approach in England, man, is incredible, it's like *Japanese!* They have this tremendous capacity for absorbing attitudes, like a big piece of wet cotton wool.

It doesn't matter what it is he's saying, it will just absorb it until it's part of the establishment. That's England's big trick. After all, didn't they do it to the Beatles? Slap a medal on them. They could never pin an MBE to the Stones, but still, all those things they put them through. . .

You only have to listen to BBC One every day to be completely in touch with what is going on in England. *Keith Richards.*

Unbelievable. It's really weird because people think of England as far more tolerant and genteel than America but when they laid that one on us, when they want to lay it down, they can be just as heavy. They just don't carry guns, that's all. *Keith Richards, 1967.*

Sex & Violence.

How come all the teenies ever wanna do is tongue my diamond tooth?
Mick Jagger, 1975.

One realises, after a while, that indiscriminate association with the opposite sex has its drawbacks.
Keith Richards.

Were you rebellious as a Teenager?
I was very emotional at that time, but then most adolescents are, like over-dramatising situations, and that's why there's always been a very big market for adolescent love songs. You know, those songs that are based on the frustrations of the adolescent. Anyone who understands that, consciously or unconsciously, and writes fantasies based on that premise gets hits.
A song like 'Young Love', which was very popular when I was around fourteen, was a heart hugging song when you were at that age. It's the same with Donny Osmond. *Mick Jagger.*

Did you have many girl-friends at that time?
Yeah. Basically the thing at that period was that you used to just try and find girls that would fuck. The rest of it was just. . . yer know. I mean, it wasn't quite as easy then as it is now. Since the invention of the Pill, it's become so much easier.
In those days, it was a big deal. You were just discovering yourself and your own body. . . kinda weird.

Were you pleased or disappointed when you first got layed?
No. I wasn't disappointed. I've always found sex very exciting, but I didn't suffer.

What kind of groupies did the Stones used to attract?
Great ugly ones – dreadful Northern ones with long black hair, plastic boots and macs. Ugh.
It used to be so terribly sordid [laughs] – still is really. Thankfully, the girls are much prettier now than they were then.

Hey, do you remember when girls nearly always seemed to have backcombed hair? I didn't like them. I used to go for the type with the straight black hair which was usually dyed. Oh God, they were so ugly.
In the States the girls were pretty good. Much younger and very clean. Not quite so rainy [laughs] not such a rainy day. *Mick Jagger,* 1974.

You can't keep it up with sixteen year old girls for ever, they're very demanding. *Mick Jagger,* 1977.

I don't go out with housewives. I never have, I'm never going to. *Mick Jagger,* 1977.

If you're gonna be a band, you can't sit in the studio the whole time. . . I'd like to do more of the only thing I can do really well, apart from screwing. *Keith Richards,* 1977.

I remember your old song 'Off The Hook': the girl's phone is always busy, you wonder what she's doing, and finally you just take your own phone off the hook. She's off the hook, but so are you.
We're all off the hook.
People seem fascinated with whether your phone is on or off the hook – in your personal life, in other words. Why do you think that is?
It's amazing to me that people want to know about my soap opera. Not just mine, of course, but mine's been a very long-running soap opera for a rock 'n' roll singer. I mean, people aren't interested in Roger Daltrey's soap opera. I'm not trying to put people down, I wish I didn't have a soap opera. Bob Dylan they're interested in now only because he's getting a divorce. Before they weren't – they didn't seem to care; he was just married and had a lot of children, and they didn't write about when he went out or whatever. No one was really *that* interested in any of the Beatles' soap operas – not to the extent that I go through it. Of course John and Yoko did get attention in the late Sixties by making an exhibition of themselves – sitting in bed, etc. But I try to avoid publicity, I'm *running.*
I don't put out wild pictures of me and whomever I'm going out with. I try to

WITH ANITA PALLENBERG AND MICHELE BRETON
IN 'PERFORMANCE', 1970

avoid going to openings as much as I possibly can. Even before I was married, with girls I was seeing or living with – most of the stories were completely untrue, and it's hopeless trying to tell people that it's not true. They'll print anything you say, anything. And by the time it gets to Hong Kong, it's ridiculous. Before you know it, you've gone out with Mrs. Trudeau, which is rubbish. The only reason I'm known in Turkey is because I'm supposed to have "gone out with Mrs. Trudeau."

I really don't like being a soap opera. It must be some sort of sexual interest. People who've got some kind of sexual attraction – and I hope I'm not being immodest by saying this – but when I was a kid I had it, I didn't have a problem getting girls. I did have a problem, though, until I started singing – I don't mind saying that. I got *nothing.* Maybe I was just shy.
Mick Jagger, 1978.

Decadence.

People bandy that word decadence about and don't know what it means. They haven't seen decadence because they can't see it in our society. They're too involved in what they are doing to see it. What do they mean by decadence – bi-sexuality? That's not decadence, but people think there is some mystique about it. It's immaterial. When people talk about

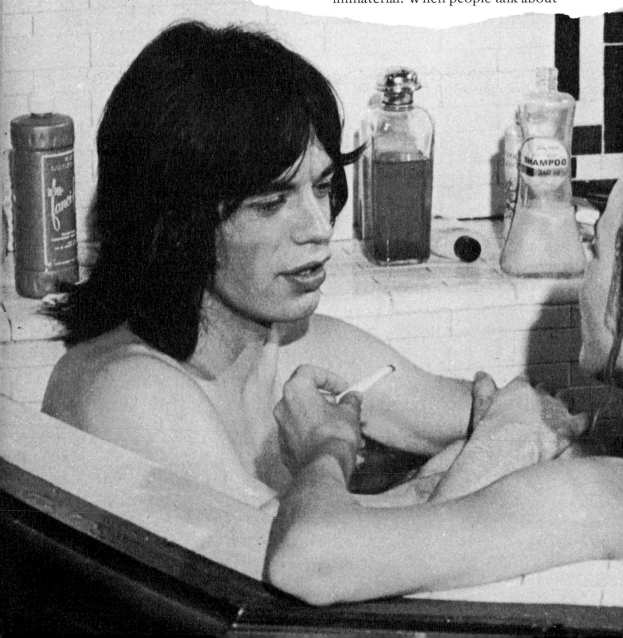

decadence, they're generally talking about *style,* especially in rock. The only person who gets accused of this so-called decadence more than me is David [Bowie]. I think David is sincere and I like what he does. It would be a lie to say his image is a hype. I think he's very talented. I don't think in three years time we'll be laughing at what he does, because he's done it better than anybody else.

Y'know, I do admire David in a way because he's doing something which a part of me would really like to do – I don't know if I can be more explicit about that but I hope you know what I mean, right. . . but at the same time. . . and Christ, it's got to a point where I daren't even wear a new pair of shoes in front of David now because he'd probably nick the idea [laughs] – I do admire him. He goes out there and. . . I've seen him do some great shows, y'know. . . like David saying he's "rewriting the script of his life" – isn't that so camp: I died when I heard that, I thought, he's just one of the lads. *Mick Jagger.*

Most of those songs are really silly, they're pretty immature. But as far as the heart of what you're saying, I'd say the same things about guys. Or if I were a girl I might say the same things about guys or other girls. I don't think any of the traits you mentioned are peculiar to girls. It's just about people. Deception, vanity. . . On the other hand, sometimes I do say rather nice things about girls [laughing].
Mick Jagger, 1978.

It's that androgynous image that seems to attract both girls and boys.

Yeah, I don't think it did in earlier years, but maybe there was always room for the androgynous type. Anyway, all guys have a feminine side. But most girls don't really fall in love with a completely gay guy, even though they like the feminine side showing. And vice versa with men. They like a woman who combines things too. They don't want someone who's either butch or totally *helpless*.

Well, there is one song that's a straight guy song – 'When The Whip Comes Down' – but I have no idea why I wrote it. It's strange – the Rolling Stones have always attracted a lot of men [laughing]. That sounds funny, but they're not all gay. And, of course, I have a lot of gay friends, but I suppose everyone does in New York City, and what's that have to do with the price of eggs. . . I don't know why I wrote it. Maybe I came out of the closet [laughing]. It's about an imaginary person who comes from L.A. to New York and becomes a garbage collector. . . But whatever: I don't like this gossip interest in me today at all. It upsets a lot of people, and it creates a lot of diversions in my life. I can ignore it in America – it's not so bad here – but in Australia and England there are so many competing gossip columns. I don't trust journalists, generally, because they don't write the truth.
Mick Jagger, 1978.

My anima is very strong. . . I think it's very kind. . . What you're saying, though, is that there are two different types of girls in my songs: there's the beautiful dreamy type and the vicious bitch type. There are also one or two others, but, yeah, you're right – there are two kinds of girls. . . only I never thought about it before.
You don't have too many girls in your songs that share both qualities.

Ah, I see, I'm not integrating them properly. Maybe not. Maybe 'Beast of Burden' is integrated slightly. I don't want a beast of burden, I don't want the kind of woman who's going to drudge for me. The song says: "I don't need a beast of burden, and I'm not going to be your beast of burden, either." Any woman can see that that's like my saying that I don't want a woman to be on her knees for me. I mean, I get accused of being very anti-girl, right?
Right.

But people really don't listen, they get it all wrong; they hear 'Beast of Burden' and say *"Arggh!" Mick Jagger,* 1978.

I'd like to ask you a personal question about 'Play with Fire.' There are lines about getting your kicks in Knightsbridge and Stepney, and a rich girl, and her father's away and there is a suggestion that the guy in the song is having an affair not only with the daughter but with the mother. . .

Ah, the imagination of teenagers! Well one always wants to have an affair with one's mother. I mean it's a turn on.
Mick Jagger.

Under Our Thumbs.

What about all those put-down songs about girls?

It was all a spinoff from our environment. . . hotels, and too many dumb chicks. Not all dumb, not by any means, but that's how one got. When you're canned up – half the time it's impossible to go out, it's a real hassle to go out – it was to go through a whole sort of football match. One just didn't. You got all you needed from room service, you sent out for it. Limousines sent tearing across cities to pick up a little bag of this or that. You're getting really cut off.
Keith Richards, 1969.

How about your woman-in-bondage poster for your 'Black and Blue' album? Many people may have a deep masochistic streak, but that poster and some of your songs certainly seem hung up on that.

Yeah, we had a lot of trouble with that particular poster. As far as the songs go, one talks about one's own experience a lot of the time. And you know, a lot of bright girls just take all of this with a pinch of salt. But there are a lot of women who *are* disgraceful, and if you just have the misfortune to have an affair with one of those. . . it's a personal thing.
And the 'squirming dog' image?

"WITH TWO LUCKY FANS", 1966

Well, that was a joke. I've never felt in that position vis-à-vis a person – I'd never want to really hurt someone.

What about the groupies on the road ready for anything? What about 'Star Star'?

Exactly! That's real, and if girls can do that, I can certainly write about it because it's what I see. I'm not saying all women are star fuckers, but I see an awful lot of them, and so I write a song called that. I mean, people show themselves up by their own behaviour, and just to describe it doesn't mean you're anti-feminist.
Mick Jagger, 1978.

Is that tour poster of the woman pointing onward supposed to represent America?

Oh, yeah, that *is* America. Onward American women is what it really means. We're for everyone to go onward. What I don't like is for these girls to get married and have a baby and get divorced and get like $350,000 and then call themselves feminists. What's that? In Central Europe, the women work and have close families and that's what *I* want.

Women's liberationists may finally accept you.
Why?

Well, because you aren't singing about stupid girls or under your thumb. You should see what happens when those songs are played at parties now. Some women really bristle.

Really? They really do? Ha ha *ha*. It's great to actually have done that, isn't it? Without realising it, right? Well, they [those songs] were really naïve – and *true*. You know? I don't think there was anything wrong with them. But when I say it, it doesn't seem to come out right. But those songs really were *true*.

In fact, there actually are such things as stupid girls?

Exactly. That's rather like saying that all black people can dance. See, what happens is that you say something and they think it applies to *all* women. Therefore they must secretly think that they were at some point – or could be – "under my thumb, there's a girl. . ." But if you really listen to the lyrics closely – not *too* closely – "under my thumb, a girl who *once* had *me* down" – you see? It's not so unfair. Why should it apply to every girl? But I think it was really true. It's funny to think about it – it was very adolescent, those songs, about adolescent experiences. There aren't any of those kind of songs, unfortunately, on this album. We have to come up with a *good* one. Soon. *Mick Jagger.*

Bad Day At Altamont.

It felt great and sounded great. I'm not used to being upstaged by Hell's Angels — goddamn it, man, somebody's motorbike. I can't believe it. For a stunt. What is the bike doing there anyway? Oh dear, a bike's got knocked over. Yes,

ALTAMONT, 1969

I perfectly understand that your bike's got knocked over, can we carry on with the concert? But they're not like that. They have a whole thing going with their bikes, as we all know now. It's like Sonny Barger, "If you've spent $1,700 . . . " *Keith Richards,* 1970.

One thing Altamont taught us was not to try and do anything like that again. In any case, rock sounds better in a room with two hundred people. It really does. *Keith Richards.*

I said I would give away any money earned from the Maysles' film of Altamont. I'm open to any suggestions. It'll probably go to some American charity of some kind. I tried to get the distribution company to give some money but they won't give a penny. Why should they, really? At least they're honest and not trying to be hypocritical about it. They just said they're in this to make money. You should take the cost of a film and then see how much it has grossed. If you think they have made five million then they should fucking well give some money. *Mick Jagger,* 1970.

At the time it was a nightmare but at the time it was just one of those "ere we go, we've gotta get through it somehow" because we can't just leave, because if we

leave, what's gonna 'appen. It taught me a lot. It taught me never to do anything I wasn't on top of. As much as I could be organisationwise, I had to do it. Never, never trust anyone else to do it for you. It was our show. Whosever fault it was, it was our fault because we weren't on top of it. You've got to be careful. *Mick Jagger,* 1974.

Somehow, in America in '69 – I don't know about now, and I never got it before – one got the feeling they really wanted to suck you out. *Keith Richards,* 1971.

Their Satanic Majesties.

When coupled with the theme of 'Jumping Jack Flash' you did take on this almost Satanic aura, didn't you?

Yeah, well that was the thing. The game, the occult. Some people are still doing it.

You know. I *am* interested in the occult, but all that was a bit silly really. Nevertheless, it's incredible the effect I had on some people just by that film, and I'm not talking about audiences. People in the film industry really thought that I was like that and they'd seen hundreds of films featuring hundreds of actors that weren't anything like the parts they portrayed. People acting as soldiers or officers but who'd never been in the army. People acting as though they were upper-class when in fact they were from the gutter.

When I came along and did that film they thought Jesus, we can never have a guy like that in a film, he's – he's a junkie Satanist.

They believed every fucking piece of it, which makes me laugh! Bloody incredible! I'll tell you, it's very difficult to do that sort of role at fucking six o'clock in the morning. *Mick Jagger,* 1974.

'Sympathy For The Devil,' that was a big drag that song.

Because of its connotations at Altamont?

Not really, It's all these young rock n' roll singers who come up to yer and say, "are you still into that devil shit? *Mick Jagger,* 1972.

Do you think of yourselves as servants of Satan?

I think there's always been an acceptance. . . I mean Kenneth Anger told me I was his right-hand man. It's just what you feel. Whether you've gotten that good and evil thing together. Left-hand path, right-hand path, how far do you want to go down?

How far?

Once you start, there's no going back. Where they lead to is another thing.

The same place?

Yeah. So what the fuck? It's something everybody ought to explore. There are possibilities there. A lot of people have played on it, and it's inside everybody. I mean, Doctor John's whole trip is based on it.

Mick and I basically have been through the same things. A lot of it comes anyway from association and press and media people laying it on people. Before, when we were just innocent kids out for a good time, they're saying, "They're evil, they're evil". Oh, I'm evil, really? So that makes you start thinking about evil.

What is evil? Half of it, I don't know how much people think of Mick as the devil or as just a good rock performer or what. There are black magicians who think we are acting as unknown agents of Lucifer and others who think we are Lucifer. Everybody's Lucifer. *Keith Richards.*

Somebody tried to lay a hex on us last year because of that. There was some incredible scheme worked out by somebody in America about letters "I" and "J". Apparently, Mick was the next.

And the cat has got some incredible story about a painting by Franz Hals, who was a Dutch warlock who painted a picture in the 16th., 17th., century of a guy playing the lute, called 'The Minstrel' or something like that – the cat looks just like Mick!

So the guy worked on these two coincidences to the point where everyone was walking around. . . [does an eyeball-rolling impression of an acid freak].

It was really amazing. I mean, his date came and went and nothing happened, but I got a copy of the painting, just to see. It's incredibly like Mick, an incredible likeness. It looks just like Jagger. Same haircut, same mouth.

But Jagger looks like several people.

Exactly, exactly. If you put a frame round the face and paint it black it'd look like Hendrix too. A wig it'd be Janis Joplin.

THE GARAGE WALL BUST, 1965

[Faint smile.] A pair of spots and it'd look like Carly Simon. *Keith Richards.*

Why do entire countries regard you as the devil incarnate?
It's convenient. . . they don't have to look any farther. I can't answer it. I've seen simple little trials – the prosecutors, for some reason it becomes so *enormous* to them, they feel they have to prove themselves. That's something to do with it, but it's not all of it, but I feel that they want to show this kid or that kid that, see that they [the prosecutors] have got some balls, that's one attitude I come across an awful lot. It's like Lenny Bruce, but – once they start on something, they don't let up, man, they just *don't.* It's very easy to pick up somebody and give them a bad name. . . There's all this incredible rivalry that goes on between different branches of the legal department even on the international scale. If the English cops can't do it, then let's show them. I guess also by popping me, they think that's worth popping 150 or 200 ordinary people. It shows people that your police are really on the ball.
Keith Richards, 1977.

Why do people practise voodoo?
All these things bunged under the name of superstition and old wives' tales. I'm no expert in it. I would never pretend to be, I just try to bring it into the open a little. There's only so much you can bring into the open. *Keith Richards,* 1971.

We piss anywhere, man. *Brian Jones,* 1965.

Bad cirumstances develop and once you get a bad reputation it's very hard to shake it off. Some bands around now get a bad reputation and that's it. It's the same in a bar. A guy has a bad reputation and he always gets picked on. One tends to get drawn into these things. From my own experience, once you've got it, you're stuck with it. This country has got to be the worst place for that. Other countries are ready to accept you may be different but take you at face value. Here they never forget anything you may have done in the past. I don't see how our image is ever going to change here. They don't want it to change, do they?
I was violent when I was younger, but most people are violent for a while when they're young, aren't they? You

have a punch-up once but you don't want a punch-up all the time, do you? I met a guy the other day I really wanted to throttle. It was at a party and I was sitting there shaking. I managed to control myself but I told him I was going to thump him. I gave him one minute to get out and he said, "Why?" *Mick Jagger, 1977.*

Any cocksucker gets caught in the wire, we *zap 'im with heavy trank. Keith Richards, 1975.*

There was nothing about love, peace and flowers in 'Jumping Jack Flash'.
Mick Jagger.

Raising A Riot.

Fucking women on stage – yuk – that's like having girls on a warship. How horrible.
Mick Jagger, 1969.

I don't understand the connection between music and violence. People are always trying to explain it to me and I just blindly carry on. I just know that I get very aroused by music, but it doesn't arouse me violently. I never went to a rock and roll show and wanted to smash the windows or beat anybody up afterwards. I feel more sexual than actually physically violent. I get a sexual feeling and I want to fuck as soon as I've been playing. I cool down very quickly. I can come off the stage and be back to normal in five minutes. You can only really get into the feeling if you're with a group of people like that. The only time I've felt violent was in some street demonstration and you really get the feeling of being in with a crowd which wants to do something and you get really carried along whether they're right or wrong. Whether the policeman is doing his job or whether the cause that you're hitting the policeman for is really right, what's it fucking matter? The point is that the act of violence is more powerful than the intellectual political act. I never felt that feeling in a crowd with music although I've felt very turned on but not like that.
Mick Jagger.

People have compared us and Andrew Oldham, to Malcolm McLaren and the Sex Pistols. But it was too obvious to work and it didn't. I'm sure Johnny Rotten realised that it was all a set-up, and went along with

it, while the others in the group couldn't think of enough swear words to keep it going!

We never did anything consciously to shock people in the days when the Stones were always in the paper. It was only other people who were shocked when we did things that had to be done.
Mick Jagger, 1977.

You ask about love . . . I believe that there is *affection*. The audience have bought tickets because they wish to see us — we are there because we like doing concerts, like audiences. There is a rapport, a tremendous, basic affection.
But on top of this affection is violence, on top of that is sex. It is a strange thing — an escalation of emotions or something. *Mick Jagger.*

It's a strange thing . . . from the audience you feel a tremendous energy. It is directed to, or at, you. It is, you feel, as if they are trying to say something to you.
But I don't know, perhaps they don't know what they are trying to say, what they want from life, or what they want from me — as a person, as a performer.
Mick Jagger.

And when the curtains part, and you see a flailing mass of waving arms, it just does something to you. Right inside. There's a swaying and a roaring. Screams? I've heard some groups say they don't like them. Well, okay for them. But we like the screams. It's all part of it, the whole proceedings, do you see? That two-way thing all over again. Sometimes that atmosphere gets real tight. It feels as if it could snap. *Brian Jones.*

I am sure that it must be a highly sexual thing. And things that are sexual are violent. *Mick Jagger.*

There was one ballroom number in Blackpool during Scots week when all the Scots come down and get really drunk and let it rip. A whole gang of them came to this ballroom and they didn't like us and they punched their way to the front, right through the whole seven thousand people, straight to the stage and started spitting at us. This guy in front spitting. His head was just football size, just right. In those days for me, I had a temper, and

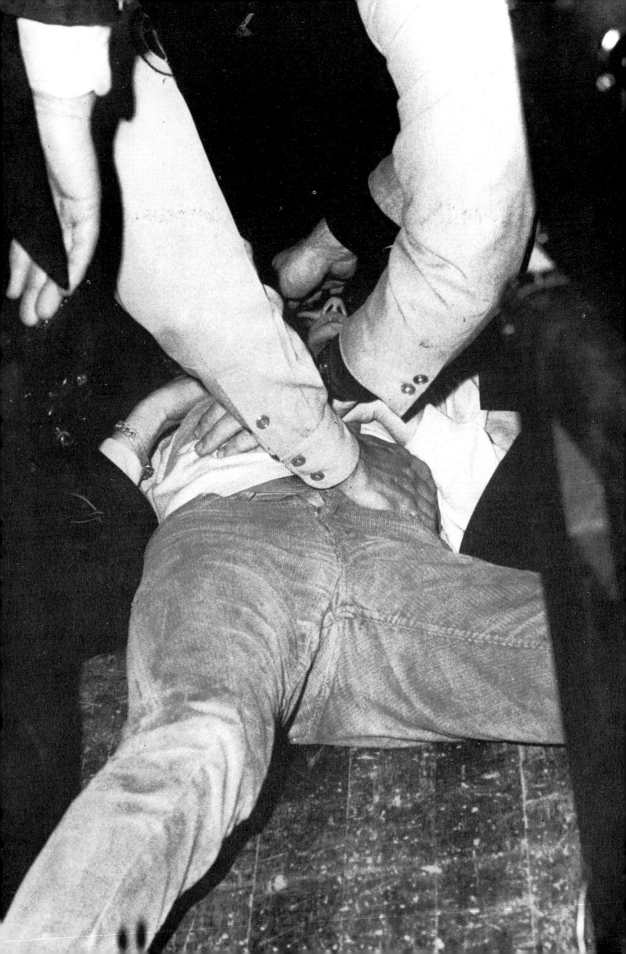

CHARLIE AFTER A COLLISION WITH A FAN, PARIS 1967/ASSOCIATED NEWSPAPERS

"You spit on me?" and I kicked his face in. It was down to the pressure of the road. *Keith Richards.*

[Explaining his black eye] Yeah, somebody threw a chair at me while we were singing. They do that sort of thing when they get excited. *Mick Jagger, 1966.*

I'm not normally frightened — though when we were in Zurich recently I was a bit scared. We were playing in a stadium — imagine somewhere with a capacity of twice London's Royal Albert Hall. We had been put on a platform thirty or forty feet above the crowd.
We walked on stage and someone jumped on my back . . . I went down like a forward under a rugger scrum. Ten of them nearly had me over the edge. Yes, I was frightened as I looked down.

Why did they do it? Oh, I suppose they thought they'd like me down there with them. *Mick Jagger.*

I got strangled twice. That's why I never wear anything around my neck any more. Going out of theatres was the dodgiest. One chick grabs one side of the chain and another chick grabs the other side . . . Another time I found myself lying in the gutter with a shirt on and half a pair of pants and the car roaring away down the street. Oh, shit, man. They leap on you. "What do you want? What?"
There was a period of six months in England we couldn't play ballrooms any more because we never got through more than three or four songs every night, man. Chaos. Police and too many people in the places fainting. *Mick Jagger.*

The recent pictures of me taken in Nazi uniform were a put-down. Really, I mean with all that long hair in a Nazi uniform, couldn't people see that it was a satirical thing? How can anyone be offended when I'm on their side? I'm not a Nazi sympathiser.
I noticed that the week after the pictures of me taken in that uniform appeared there were photographs of Peter O'Toole in the same newspaper wearing a German uniform for a film he's making. But no one put him down for wearing that. *Brian Jones, 1966.*

Half the reason for going out at night is still to find a bit of bovver. Probably even more so now that a lot of them have got no job and probably never had a job. It must be weird after a while. If you've been unemployed four or five years after coming out of school, if they ever find you a job, you've been in such a different thing for five years that you can no longer live that way of life. *Keith Richards, 1976.*

Do you think people have been frightened of me? Perhaps you're right. I'd like to do some more films someday and people keep on offering me nasty roles. They reckon I've got an evil face. *Mick Jagger, 1977.*

What a terrible monster I am. I feel guilty about it afterwards, then I laugh, because the whole thing is a joke. But Keith is worse than I am. Is he a prima donna? Oh yeah. *Mick Jagger, 1977.*

The Politics Of Delinquency.

The trouble is that people get a buzz out of being reviled. They listen to something and say "Wasn't that revolting? Let's listen to it again!" Now if they are so reviled, they don't have to listen to it. They can turn it off or not play or not buy the record. But why should they tell everyone else what they should do?

They told me that 'Street Fighting Man' was subversive. "Of course it's subversive," we said. It's stupid to think that you can start a revolution with a record. I wish you could! *Mick Jagger, 1970.*

The song itself is the only thing that has to do with street fighting.

You sing of politics, protest and revolution.

Oh, no, I don't sing of revolution.

In your song, 'Street Fighting Man' it says "The time is right for fighting in the street."

But it then says, "But what can a poor boy do, except sing in a rock 'n' roll band" – what else can I do besides sing?

Do you really think it's appropriate not to sing about the revolution?

We don't do that. In America, the rock 'n' roll bands have gotten very political. They express themselves very directly about the Vietnam war. But when I come home to England, everything is completely different, so quiet and peaceful. If one lives in such an atmosphere, one has a great detachment from politics and writes completely different about them. *Mick Jagger, 1969.*

How many times can you use those words – justice, freedom. It's like margarine, man. You can package it and you can sell that too. In America they have a great talent for doing that.

And so, as I was saying, just because it's on a record doesn't mean that you have to take it for what it is. The cat could be lying, you know, at the end of the record, you know, maybe they cut the tape off and he said, "Oh, I'm sorry, I'm lying. You know, I'm just fooling you." But they just happened to edit the tape there, you know. "I'm putting you on."

Maybe Dylan said at the end of 'Visions of Johanna' – oh, I don't know, which is a very personal thing – but maybe he said it at the end of some of his earlier stuff: "But I don't give a fuck," at the end of 'Blowin' In The Wind' or 'That's Up To You,' maybe he said that. *Keith Richards, 1971.*

If I'd been a French rock 'n' roll singer, I'm sure we'd all have been very involved in the revolution in France. Put in that position we'd probably have thrown all to the winds and been there at the barricades, so to speak. But in England it's always terribly difficult to see, to find out where the barricades are. The barricades are just clowns. *Mick Jagger, 1969.*

There's always people trying to look too deeply into the words. They'd like to let rip but they get caught up with mentions of President Kennedy or those little devil things. Just the mention of revolution sends them wondering. *Ron Wood, 1975.*

As They See Us.

For us it's a big drag. No one quite throws their hands up in horror at us anymore, but we do object to the politics of it. We feel that our right to be able to play where we want to and when we want to is being consciously interfered with.

No one else gets the hassles we get and we don't do anything no one else doesn't do.

It's never just the Palm Court Orchestra in town to play for the night. You can't divorce the music entirely from the scene that it's all built on. It's all part of "the Stones are the Stones, warts and all."

The daily media's horror of rock

ANDREW LOOG OLDHAM AND
KEITH RICHARDS, 1966/MICHAEL COOPER

groups seems to begin and end with us. They don't get excited about anybody else's excesses as much. [A shrug of resignation] I guess you can only have one bad boy at a time, really, and we're it.

There's not really much you can do about it. They can print what they like about us because people believe it, anyway.

It amuses me personally, but on another level it's kind of frightening – the generalisations they can make without anybody apparently having to take any responsibility for it.

Did you feel this incredible pressure from the establishment weighing upon you?

God, no! If I felt it, man, I'd just give up and go away! I'm not unconscious of it but. . . I don't feel there's any kind of weight. It seems that the press turn you into what they want you to be, and as far as the people are concerned that's what you are. *Keith Richards.*

As We See Them.

Do you think there is really a global conspiracy against the Rolling Stones?

Naw, I'd just call it us *vs* them. It's *all* political whatever you wanna call it. I'll take my chances on the outside. We'll just keep on doin' it our way.

And on their side there's this . . . well, not exactly a conspiracy, but it does become that.

Once you plant some idea in people's minds there doesn't have to be. The conspiratorial element is there. Once you've got the idea underlying they can re-use it, and that is a conspiracy.

Great emphasis was placed by the Establishment on the supposed yobbo image of the Stones . . .

There still is, dear, [laughs]. There's not a lot of difference.

Was this by accident or intent and how much did Andrew contribute to perpetuating this imagery?

That was his job. What was he there for if not to publicise the band? It's every fucking manager's job to control the media. We really did want to be stars, that's why I don't really regret anything.

Did you ever find yourselves feeling everything was going wrong?

Oh yeah, because they were going completely the wrong way around 1964, the beginning of '65.

When we first went to America I thought, this isn't what it's really all about and not what we're supposed to do. We had these recurring crises in the band

MICK JAGGER AND KEITH RICHARDS/MICHAEL COOPER

about what we were supposed to be doing in relationship to what we originally set out to do – what we hadn't done with regard to what we had done.

When it became commonplace for JP's, MP's and other 'civil dignitaries' to put the Stones publicly down as a bad influence on teenagers, what was your reaction?

We thought it was hilarious. It was just publicity and we didn't even have to bother to go along with it, it just sorta happened outside of us.

When you get the ball going they do it all for you, especially in this country. You don't have to do a thing, the media will pick up on it and exaggerate it beyond recognition. If they just get so much as a smell of a story they'll make it up or get a quote and turn it around to suit themselves.

I don't have to tell you . . . the media need a story and the bands need to be publicised. *Mick Jagger.*

In Russia we've tried very hard. And we've received a lot of rebuffs. But there's a genuine demand for the band in Russia, that I know. In China, though, I should think there's absolutely zero. In Russia, there's a genuine knowledge of western music — jazz, rock, all types. Eastern Europe, everyone's been over there, all

the English bands go there, but they're severely restricted. They wouldn't let us in, we're going to freak them out with some fucking weird show.

If we went to Russia, I'd like to go with Stevie Wonder, you know, and a whole bunch of people, not just the Rolling Stones. We'd like a week in Moscow, and we'd take everything: all the techniques we've learned, all the lights, everything we've learned about different types of music. And we'd just show them what we've done and if they don't like it, too bad. But at least we've done it, you know? Those countries I'm not just thinking about for the Stones but for the whole . . . music of now, which in some sense we can help. *Mick Jagger,* 1975.

Aw, c'mon Mick, what would Japanese politicians possibly have to gain from refusing the Stones entry visas?

Why? Ask the inscrutable face. There were a lot of people who wanted to see us. They'd given us permission to play and that's why we'd put the tickets on sale. We'd made the stage, painted the scenery and two weeks before we were supposed to go they turned round and said we couldn't. We said "thank you, have some raw fish."

They said it was because of the bust, but they've let people in who've had busts.

It's all politics – we're just a football in

the middle really. It's ridiculous that it should all get to such a high level; it was the same with Australia – they had a change of government which fortunately for us said "give it a whirl" so we went this year. Big deal.

Politically, people on the lower rungs think they may get into trouble if they let us in, then they turn to someone higher up and so it goes on. That's what happened in Australia until the Prime Minister had the final say, which is totally absurd when he gets involved. And yet they wouldn't let Chip Monck in to do the sets for us, although he'd been there for months doing all the reccies.

One's got a right as a musician to work, but between the governments, the immigration and the unions who are supposed to help you work, you don't get very far. I don't think the Musician's Union in this country has ever helped anybody. No doubt upon reading this that they'll drag out one case from 1964 or something.

And our trouble is that whatever we do everybody wants a slice of the action. If you go out and earn twenty grand at a gig they reckon they're entitled to a bit, despite the fact they've done absolutely nothing. *Mick Jagger.*

On tours, we go around like nomads on these well-beaten tracks. I mean, there's people *screaming* for it. It's like BP [British Petroleum] not going and tapping some huge oil field, you know, just not bothering. Can you imagine that? It's equivalent, the audiences. They'd be down there like a shot after the pipelines. Rock 'n' roll is ignored. There are thousands and thousands of record buyers. They should be knocking on Moscow's fucking door, they should be hitchhiking down to South America. You could go to New Delhi or Calcutta, there are thousands of street kids there. Africa has got to be another place where we could get it together.

In Russia they spend so many roubles on black market records, and there's a very big scene in South America but when you try to do a tour there you run into so many problems. There's not enough people experienced enough to guarantee that you're going to get out, or get a show on. There's not enough experienced crews from our part of the world who speak Portuguese or Spanish.

I mean if Leningrad is going to go

potty over *Cliff* Richard . . . In towns like Bratislava there are these posters in the street of rock 'n' roll stars, completely music crazy, then the tanks came in and that was it.

All these governments, though, all they can think about is drug convictions, drug arrests, drugs. Right?

Yeah. I think they are just scared of association or whatever. I can't believe that a government would spend two seconds of its time worrying about what rock 'n' roll band is coming to its country. But they do . . . The idea is: "Let's grab *him?*" So it just becomes political outlaws – there really isn't any way for anybody in our position or my position to get a fair trial, because of the image, or the prejudice, anything, anyway. It's already against me just because of the image . . . *illegal*, they are really out to make rock 'n' roll illegal.

Really, it would be illegal to play the goddamn music, that's the basic drive behind that whole thing. They are just scared of that rhythm. Certainly every sound has an effect on the body and the effects of a good backbeat makes these people shiver in their boots, so you are fighting some primeval fear that you can't even rationalise, because it's to do with the chromosomes and the exploding genes.

But you have had a lot to do with it, with songs like 'Satisfaction' and 'Street Fighting Man,' which don't lose their impact on an audience.

Songs – yeah. People think you're a songwriter, they thing you wrote it, it's all yours, you are totally responsible for it. Really, you are just a medium, you just develop a facility for recognising and picking up things and you just have to be ready to be there – like being at a seance; they just plop out of the air. Whole songs just come to you, you don't write it. Songs come to me en masse, I didn't do anything except to happen to have been awake when it arrived. *Keith Richards,* 1977.

The music says something very basic and simple, man . . . which, I don't know, exasperates. I mean, look at Richard Nixon and then look at your average young cat in the street, or some Indian cat. It's all there, you've only got to look at what's in front of you. And that's all we've ever been trying to do. Not trying to tell people where to go or which way to go because I don't know. We're all following. I mean, it's all going to happen. It's all coming down.

And to us it might seem, oh, world population. Before there were newspapers and radios and TV you wouldn't hear about that. You would never hear about that plague in India or Bengal that they're having and the cholera thing. If you were living in Wales at the time of the great plague in London you probably wouldn't get to hear about that until five years after it happened. And so, something like world population, you wouldn't even know about it.

Depends how worried you want to get about everything. I mean, how can you worry about world population, whose problem is that? You tell me. Everybody feels they ought to do something about it. If you know the facts. On the face of it it sounds scary. But after a while it always splits into two things, one side is, "Oh, in ten years there's going to be so many people on the earth and you're not going to be able to do this, that and the other," and the other says, "Oh yes; it's going to be terrible for them, but it's going to be all right for us." And then there's "Oh, the world's growing too much food and they're just throwing it all away, enough to feed the world five times over is being thrown into the Atlantic Ocean," and the only reason it's not getting to the people that need it to stay alive is either because they don't want to afford the cost of transporting it to those people or they want those people to die anyway. I mean, what about the tidal wave in Pakistan, man? Quarter of a million in one night.

I'll just keep on rocking and hope for the best. I mean, that's really what in all honesty it comes down to. I mean, why do people want to be entertainers or do they want to listen to music or come and watch people make music? Is it just a distraction or is it a vision or God knows what? It's everything to all kinds of people. You know, it's all different things. *Keith Richards, 1969.*

Some people try and reflect it, don't they? Crosby, Stills, Nash and Young? The song, 'Chicago'—like that.

Good topical stuff.

Which sells records?

Certainly. Mayor Daley's a good target. And there's a million Daleys in America. Why have a go at one? Sure he's a cunt, you know, everyone knows he's a cunt. But there's a million hiding behind. Last time I was in L. A. I met the old lady that owns most of those head shops in the Strip, man. She's got a little home in Beverly Hills, she's rolling, you know. She's made a packet, man and she gets those little hippies to work in there. And it's a front, man. It's all a fucking front. There's another Mayor Daley. *Keith Richards, 1969.*

Who knows, man? I mean they used to put it down so heavy, rock 'n' roll. I wonder if they knew there was some rhythm in there that was gonna shake their house down. *Keith Richards, 1971.*

After 1967, you were suddenly the bad boys?

Yeah. It kind of said, "OK, from now on it's heavy." Up till then, it had been showbiz, entertainment, play it how you want to, teenyboppers. At that point you knew, they considered you to be outside . . . they're the ones, who put you outside the law. Like Dylan says, "To live outside the law, you must be honest."

They're the ones that decide who lives outside the law. I mean, you don't decide, right? You're just livin'. I mean your laws don't apply to me, nobody says that, because you can't. But they say it. And then you have to decide what you're going to do from then on. *Keith Richards.*

The government? One always finishes up with the lesser of two evils. Really, I'm an anarchist. Colour prejudice? Makes me sick. We've travelled a lot in the past year or so and some of the things I've seen have made me realise what a big problem it is. You've got to experience it to know what it's all about. America? They're enjoying a standard of living that we'll probably get in fifty years. *Brian Jones.*

No, I'm not a nihilist. I don't know. I'm not really going through a very spiritual phase at the moment, I must say. I seem to have been going through a totally physical phase. I think you should build upon your spiritual life as much as you can, it's really important. Nearly everybody avoids it, because it's painful, you know? It's really the end of one's life to build your spiritual life to the highest peak, and that's what I really aim to do with my life. Anyway, doesn't mean it's going to apply to everybody. *Mick Jagger, 1977.*

The Music.

Well, that's because we're playing better than the other groups. Your original precept, though, that rock's not going anywhere – you're like one of those old jazz people who say jazz doesn't exist after death of Bix Beiderbecke. I think that rock 'n' roll will go on and slowly change forms but it's always had the basic form, the basic, basic form.

But that's also its limitation, because it's dance music.

Yeah, yeah, strong backbeat, it's primitive. You can go on upward and outward but you have to come back to that. I just say music is *music* because I'm not trained musically. If I was trained, I would write really good things that I can't write. I *could* write a symphony. I'm not interested in just playing rock 'n' roll, as rock 'n' roll is defined by rock 'n' roll writers. I like African music, Cajun music – whatever makes me dance.

Well, Mick, is rock progressing or is it static?

I don't wanta argue about it, I just wanta say that I don't really care. Because all music to me is the *same*. Ever since I played music, I never defined it. Now Brian Jones defined it as R'n'B, that's *blues* and *that's* rock & roll. And to a certain extent *that* was the Rolling Stones. But after that I refused to define it, so it's all music to me – country, R&B – they're popular music, *folk* music, call it what you will, but don't talk about strict rock 'n' roll.

Rock 'n' roll is really just like the show this evening. When jazz came out, right, at the turn of the century, coloured people had this kind of music and it took much longer for white people to play it, with some exceptions, right? It took till the Fifties for white people to make a success out of rhythm & blues, a success out of black people. It was very quick, it was an explosion. Now you can see – the Stones are not creating anything new, personally, that I can see. But we don't know for sure, *that's* the adventure. *Mick Jagger, 1978.*

It's my job, playin' music. My vocation. No musician is beyond that . . . until he gets too old. There's a certain magic in

repetition . . . but that's a dead subject. *Mick Jagger, 1975.*

Keith Richards once said something to the effect that rock 'n' roll really is subversive because the rhythms alter your being and perceptions. With your words and your rhythms, your stuff could do, and has done that, don't you think?

Rhythms are very important. But subvert what?

Well, Keith Richards' implication was that words could be used to lie, but that what the Stones did was just to let you see clearly the way things were. And that that *vision – or so I inferred – was not what was subversive.*

Maybe Keith did mean that. Music is one of the things that changes society. That old idea of not letting white children listen to black music is *true*, 'cause if you want white children to remain what they are, they musn't.

Look at what happened to you [laughing].

Exactly! You get different attitudes to things . . . even the way you walk . . .

And the way you talk.

Right, and the way you talk. Remember the Twenties when jazz in Europe changed a lot of things. People got more crazy, girls lifted up their dresses and cut their hair. People started to dance to that music, and it made profound changes in that society. . . This sounds awfully serious! *Mick Jagger.*

I don't think rock 'n' roll should be analysed or even thought about deeply.

Y'see . . . rock 'n' roll is only any good when you're confident about it. Hesitate and you're lost, especially on stage. *Keith Richards.*

I've never really liked what goes for white rock and roll, you know. Never ever, come to that. Speaking as one white person to another [smirk], no, I just can't dance to it. I find it very, very difficult to dance to white people playing because they get all the, uh, accents wrong. It's not even that it's too fast, it's just that all the accents are in the wrong places. I mean, I've really always felt like that about white rock – from Elvis to the Sex Pistols – and I'm not going to stop thinking that way because of any new band. *Mick Jagger, 1977.*

I can also understand when people say that certain artists have been around far too long, but I think that happens more in America than over here. You see, new bands coming up with kids all from the same neighbourhood doesn't seem to happen much any more. Everything is far too manufactured, just like the jazz idea of putting together all-star bands, and it's because of this I don't think rock and roll is going to last much longer. *Mick Jagger.*

The Lyrics.

I think that rock and roll songs are pretty ephemeral. To me they are because when I've done one I want to write another one. I think that as soon as you've recorded a song it doesn't belong to you any more. It just goes out and everyone can sing it, everyone can do it if they want. They can change it. You know what I mean? It's not yours. It's yours when you are playing it in your bedroom or something, it's still private, but when you've let it out you've got to get on with something else. *Mick Jagger, 1974.*

The songs we're writing cannot be compared with those by Cole Porter, Irving Berlin or Rodgers and Hammerstein. They were written for the sophisticated. Their songs are now called standards – they're old songs, that's all. Written for people of 25 to 30 about an age that has mostly passed. You play something long enough and often enough and everyone says it's a standard – 'Long Tall Sally' must be a standard now. *Mick Jagger.*

When someone in a tuxedo with greasy hair like Frank Sinatra comes along and records one of our songs then maybe we'll have a standard, too. The Irving Berlin type of music was founded on a basis of light opera and jazz. Our music is drawn from the influences of white and negro folk music. We try to reflect forward looking attitudes. You have to be progressive when you write for young people. *Keith Richards.*

Have you ever taken a tale, say, and stretched it into, say, a short story?
Needless to say, no. It's quite a good

idea to do if you've got the kernel of a good story. It's very hard, actually – unless you're really good – to get any kind of narrative into a song of four and a half minutes. It's so complicated: "And *then* he . . . " If it got as complicated as it could have been, it would really have got boring. And the thing is to *not* say a lot.
And also make it rhyme?
Making it *rhyme?* We don't have to worry about making it *rhyme.*
Mick Jagger, 1976.

Often times when you record, you mumble your lyrics. Is this done purposely as a style?
That's when the bad lines come up. I mean I don't think the lyrics are that important. I remember when I was very young, this is very serious. I read an article by Fats Domino which has really influenced me. He said "you should never sing the lyrics out very clearly."

You can really hear "I got my thrill on Blueberry Hill."
Exactly, but that's the only thing you can hear just like you hear "I can't get no satisfaction." It's true what he said though. I used to have great fun deciphering lyrics. I don't try to make them so obscure that nobody can understand but on the other hand I don't try not to. I just do it as it comes. *Mick Jagger, 1966.*

The Songwriters.

Future? Know something? I never even think about it. Today's what counts. Ambitions? Things are fine now. But I want to keep on writing songs with Mick. It's a good partnership, I think – we never seem to be short of ideas.
Keith Richards, 1966.

Who was writing what songs?
Well, I used to write nearly all the words in that period. That was my contribution, though quite often Keith used to write the words until 'Between The Buttons.' And then, in a very modest way, I started writing the tunes as well.
'Angie' is kind of a throw-back to the 'Back Street Girl.' 'Lady Jane.' 'You Better Move On' ballads which we used to do. We've always done that and they've always come off. If the song has been halfway good we somehow always manage to sell. I don't always want to come off with a rocker. It's important to try and do

Whereas Keith prefers to be more spontaneous.
[Chews on the thought] No, I wouldn't call it spontaneous if you've been there for ten hours on one riff. [Makes a face of mock disgust] 'E just goes in there with a riff and if nothing 'appens he goes back the next day. It's all right for 'im. I have to write the tune! *Mick Jagger.*

Between you and Keith, who is the more experimentally inclined?
Well, in a partnership one of you has to be. I'm just as much a rock 'n' roller as Keith, but one of you has to be that way else it'd be too much for people to take.
I don't like people saying "this one is mine!" It doesn't matter what anyone fucking says. Then you get in the position of wanting to be known for your greatness. As long as you can work with someone to bounce off. You can't bounce off yer old lady like you can yer songwriter. *Mick Jagger.*

I only know one way to work, and this is true for me and Mick J. both, and that's to carry on until it sounds right.
As soon as you stop retouching, or re-recording on the grounds that like, 90 per cent of the people ain't gonna know the difference anyway, then you're really lost. *Keith Richards.*

I've learned a lot from Keith. I could go into the studio and make a Rolling Stones type album, not archetypal Stones music perhaps, but then who needs that all the time? But then again I've always said that Keith could go in by himself and make a great studio album. I believe he could, too. *Mick Jagger,* 1968.

I couldn't do what I do better in another band. Sometimes I might record the odd song alone, but that's the way we've always worked. Mick might say to me: "Your rough tape has got the best feel, why don't you do that one." But we still work closely on songs. It still comes together even when we haven't seen each other for months. We help each other on songs like 'Miss You' which came together during the 1976 tour of Europe. A lot of our songs take a long time to come out. I thought *Some Girls* was the most immediate album we had done in a long while and you can't argue with seven million sales. It took off just at the right period in the band's evolution. *Keith Richards,* 1979.

something else. So that's why we did 'Angie'. I suppose it didn't come off so well in some places, but it did come off pretty well around the world. *Mick Jagger,* 1977.

Even though you had several hits before, 'Satisfaction' was really the turn on for a vast majority of people. Was there any specific incident that brought those lyrics to you?
It was Keith really. I mean it was his initial idea. It sounded like a folk song when we first started working on it and Keith didn't like it much, he didn't want it to be a single, he didn't think it would do very well. That's the only time we have had a disagreement.

Even when it was finished, he didn't like it?
I think Keith thought it was a bit basic. I don't think he really listened to it properly. He was too close to it and just felt it was a silly kind of riff. *Mick Jagger,* 1968.

But you and Keith do occasionally write songs separately?
'Sympathy For The Devil,' I wrote that – but it's a bit of a bore going through who wrote all the songs 'cos I have to think about it. *Mick Jagger,* 1977.

I hear it takes the two of you ages to write a number.
'Oo you 'earing all this from then? You gettin' these impressions from out of the air? [grinning at his own sarcasm]. It's balls. No, I write 'undreds every day. Writing 'em all the time, I am.
Is it true you like to go into the studio with everything planned out, or at least worked on.

Brian never wrote a single finished song in his life. His paranoia was far too great. *Keith Richards.*

He never played me a song he had written so it's quite hard to know what he wanted to do. He was very shy and that and I think he found it hard to lay it down to us, this was a song and it went like this. And we probably sort of didn't think to draw it out of him probably which is I suppose a bit insensitive of us. *Mick Jagger,* 1974.

How did you get one of your original compositions, 'In Another Land,' on Their Satanic Majesties Request?

The only reason that went on the album was because on the night that it was recorded, Charlie and I were the only ones who turned up for the session. Glyn Johns was engineering those sessions, and they seemed to go on forever because the drug busts were on and we didn't know whether Mick and Keith were going to prison for God knows how long or what. Mick was maybe getting three years and Keith was getting a year– we didn't know. They were out on bail and there were appeals, and the tour had been cancelled. It was a very, very weird time about then. So on this particular night, I turned up as usual and Glyn told me one night, you've forgotten it and have to start all over again. But it's the way we record, and it seems to work.

Do you hope to write more songs for the Stones?

Basically, there's not really any room for another songwriter in our band. I'd like to be involved if I could, and I'm sure Ronnie Wood would. And Mick Taylor definitely wanted to be, which was one of his frustrations. So it's a little bit of a drag, but if you only record one album every eighteen months or so, which is what we've done for the last eight years, there's not much room for anyone else. By the time we get around to recording, Mick and Keith have so many songs ready that they have to weed tunes out. Besides, the kind of things I write may not be the right kind of songs for the Stones. *Bill Wyman.*

Over the years, Mick and Keith have written so many excellent songs that there's really no room for anyone else in the band to write. They know precisely what they're doing. Truthfully, I have no desire to do my own music within the context of the Stones. Even if we were on

the road and my album went gold, I'd never perform one of my own songs on a Rolling Stones show– it's got absolutely nothing to do with the group. *Bill Wyman,* 1976.

The Method.

What is your procedure when you're putting together an album?

I just go in there with a germ of an idea, the smaller the germ the better, and give it to them, feed it to them, and see what happens. Then it comes out as a Rolling Stones record instead of me telling everybody what I want them to play. That way no one's got any preconceived ideas. All they've got is a notion to go on.

Which is exactly what Keith Richards is, a notion to go on. Which is exactly why their records sound like group efforts united by a common feel.

The band can work it out any way they want. If it works great, if it doesn't happen I know I can go in there the next night with another germ. I know I'm gonna grab them some way, infect them somehow. If it's a good track Mick and I can finish it off, polish it up.

There are songs that start off as my particular riff, but they get taken up by others in the band and turned into something I didn't imagine. Whereas something like 'Angie' turned out pretty much as I expected. Which was another reason why on 'Let It Bleed' we put that other version of 'Honky Tonk Women' on 'cause that's how I wrote it, as a real Hank Williams/Jimmy Rodgers/Thirties country song. And it got turned around to this

other thing by Mick Taylor who got into a completely different feel throwing it off the wall another way.

Group strength has slid off that wall like putty and refused to go away, bouncing back in different shapes and forms recognisable because they all place rhythm above lead.

As long as the bass and drums have got a groove going from the minute the record starts till the end, I don't give a damn what anybody else is playing 'cause they can rub it off and overdub. As long as that rhythm section is *there* – you can do anything. If I'm right along with them it helps even more.

But recording is such a personal thing for me, anyhow . . .

How much of the album is written before you go into the studio?

Very, very little. I might take in a few ideas on tape, a few preliminary cassettes, but most of it happens there and then.

In between albums, we've all travelled, right? And we pick up ideas from all over and and kick them around in the studio; maybe laying down a few nervous and hesitant tracks to start off. . . it's fucking expensive recording this way, I might add! . . . and I generally find that I'll be able to write a song after the first few days, using the rough tracks as a basis.

From there, it all falls into place, hopefully. And the first couple of songs shape the direction and the nature of the album.

I don't like to work completely haphazard. If things are gonna fall into place, they've got to fall into place properly. Songs tend to come together quickly, or else they don't come together at all.

We have to know what we're gonna be singing about to start off. And we'll work from a title perhaps or from a line of Mick's.

Don't you ever work the other way, like for instance hit upon some neat riff and organise a song around that?

No. If you try and add a melody to a riff rather than it evolving from it, it always sounds completely false, like the melody's been stuck on the top with a piece of Sellotape.
Keith Richards.

When we're recording it's not a question of getting it over quickly. It's getting a take which the majority likes. You can imagine,

this tends to take much longer than it did when we first started. The consolation is that these days our records sound so much better.

As far as I'm concerned, once I've done my bit there's nothing else for me to do except hang about the studio. It's O.K. if the boys have brought some people in to do some overdubs or the girls are doing a back-up vocal track – otherwise it's just boring. *Charlie Watts,* 1973.

Studios are like airports. They're all the same. It's always a shock to me when I walk out of a studio and suddenly realise I'm in Jamaica, Munich, Los Angeles. *Keith Richards,* 1976.

But why five string guitars?

There's no big secret, or mystery attached to them at all. They're tuned the same as a five-string banjo and that's a great tuning for playing slide guitar in.

Robert Johnson used to use it on acoustic and there's a lot of his riffs that I play that don't work at all in conventional tuning.

And for rhythm work. . . ordinarily, when you change chords, the previous chord is completely dead. With the five string, you get kind of a drone going all the way through. *Keith Richards,* 1974.

When we recorded the first album, two track was 'it.' Now everything sounds so clean and sanitized like a supermarket, all hygienically wrapped, unless you work hard to get what you're doing exactly how you want it to sound. It's a constant battle with technology. You welcome whatever they come up with, as it widens possibilities of what you can do, but it closes the door on what was possible before.

That's why I started recording on cassettes. 'Street Fighting Man' and 'Jumpin Jack Flash' were all supposed to be done in a reaction to 8 track. At that time I was just fed up with everything coming out. The thing I've got to complain about modern technology is that with more and more tracks every year it tends to make every band sound the same. Too much technology makes it more and more difficult to record rock 'n' roll properly. I had to stop recording on cassettes once they started putting limiters on them but now you can bypass the limiter so I may start using them again. I record a lot at

Ronnie Wood's home-built studio. It's almost Back-To-Mono. There's only eight tracks which is fine by me. Eight tracks keep you at it, you can't afford to waste tracks. Ronnie's studio is a gas. It's small, but somehow you don't get that claustrophobic feeling that always hits you in Studio Number Two.
Keith Richards, 1974.

But I refuse to get too refined about making records. I like the earthy approach to rock 'n' roll, which is why the Stones aren't real different from me. They've been saying all along what I've been trying to get at. *Ron Wood,* 1979.

The Albums.

Whose decision was it to record 'Come On' as the Stones debut single?
Ours. Nobody else knew it and to the best of our knowledge nobody had done it. I don't think it was very good, in fact it was shit. . . It really was shit. God knows how it ever got in the charts, it was such a hype.
In fact we disliked it so much we didn't do it on any of our gigs. I remember playing at the Scene Club in Ham Yard that Ronan O'Reilly used to run. It was quite a nice club – anyway, Andrew came down and watched the set and we didn't do 'Come On' which was our record at the time, and he said why didn't we play it, and we told him that we didn't really like it.
You gotta do it, he yelled. He didn't want to know that we thought it was horrible. Eventually we did it in the ballrooms and the people seemed to dig it.
Keith was quoted as saying that quite a number of tracks on the first album were just demos or unfinished tracks.
I don't remember it being like that. There were a couple of demos on it. 'Tell Me' was one of them.
There are some nice things on 'Between The Buttons'
Well. I never really liked. . . Well, tell me one [pleads] – just one song.
O.K. then, 'Back Street Girl'?
That's the only decent song. The rest of it is more or less rubbish, Oh yes, there *is* another one that's good called 'Connection' which is more or less Keith on his own.
Yeah, that's a good one, but other than that it's a terrible album. That's when I started getting out of the pop thing and leaving all that behind. *Mick Jagger,* 1974.

Satanic Majesties seems like a real oddity in the Stones career.
'Satanic Majesties' was the mood of the times. In those times it was flowers, beads and stars on yer face, that's what it was.
You can't play or write outside the mood of the times, unless you live on a mountain – and even in the South of France I wasn't that out of it even if I couldn't get the *Melody Maker.*
In fact, I'm rather fond of that album, and I wouldn't mind doing something like that again. *Mick Jagger,* 1974.

Goats Head Soup, that was just a making-time album. *Keith Richards,* 1977.

Rehearsing guitar players, that's what that one [*Black and Blue*] was about.
Keith Richards, 1977.

[Listening to *Hot Stuff* on the turntable] don't you think we sound a little like the Ohio Players on that one?
Mick Jagger, 1976.

We are progressive in our own way. If you run back through the albums I don't think you'll find that we have repeated ourselves. And that is progression. We have cut tracks lately which have been experimental and that's progression for us. It's also progression for the Stones to play a good country song, or give a country song a new twist, or a rock song a new life. *Mick Jagger,* 1966.

How much of a creative influence was Oldham on the Stones?
I don't really know. I'd have to go through all the records one by one to answer that.
He had some influence – but on what is a different matter. It was not so much on what numbers we did, but that he helped to get the whole thing going, making sure things were done and encouraging us.
It was Andrew who encouraged us to write. Our first song was 'It Should Be You' and was recorded by George Bean on Decca . . . the late George Bean. Actually he was quite a nice bloke.
Mick Jagger, 1974.

If you really go into each album there's always something that represents each of our periods.
We don't do it intentionally. Like

saying let's go into the studio and do something we used to do around '64 and then something we did in '67. But it does work out like that. An album or a single only represents the mood you were in at the time it was written and recorded.

Say, if you're madly in love with some chick and you're touring America, or say you're very lonely or anything, and you write a whole bunch of songs to record – you're never ever going to re-create that mood once you've come back to London in the middle of winter. You're not going to write those songs again. . .

Songwriting and playing is a mood.

Like the last album we did was basically recorded in short concentrated periods. Two weeks here two weeks there – then another two weeks. And, similarly, all the writing was concentrated so that you get the feel of one particular period of time. Three months later it's all very different and we won't be writing the same kind of material as 'Goat's Head Soup.'

What I'm saying is that you can write and play to order. *Mick Jagger,* 1974.

I'm not interested in solo albums. All these bands splintering up for individual members to record their own stuff seems pointless. First you come up against the problem of whether to hold back your best material for your album or the band's next effort. I suppose in a few isolated cases it's relevant but . . . I mean, there are thousands of good musicians but that's as far as it goes, really. It takes more than just musicianship to substantiate a whole album. *Keith Richards,* 1975.

Both the Beatles and us had been through buying albums that were filled with ten tracks of rubbish. We said, "No, we want to make each track good. Work almost as hard on it as you would work on a single.' So maybe we changed that concept.

Still, we were on the road every night

RECORDING WITH ANDREW LOOG OLDHAM, 1963/CYRUS ANDREWS

so there are probably a couple of tracks in there that are probably bummers because Andrew said, "Well, put that on." Because up until the Beatles and ourselves got into records, the cat who was singing had absolutely no control, man. None at all. He had no say in the studio. The backing track was laid down by session men, under the A and R man, artists and repertoire, whatever the fuck that means. He controlled the artist and the material. Bobby Vee or Billy Fury just laid down the vocal. They weren't allowed to go into the booth and say, "I want my voice to sound like this, or I want the guitar to sound like this." The man from the record company decided what went where.

That's why there became longer and longer gaps between albums coming out because we got into trying to make everything good. *Keith Richards,* 1971.

There was a point at which we decided that we just won't play, we're just making records. We weren't playing at all. We can sit down and play *that* song from *that* album if necessary, you know what I mean? Because there are all sorts of songs that we can play, but there was a point where we couldn't. "Could you do some of those tracks from 'Satanic Majesties?' And I couldn't remember how they'd go. That was just like the studio stuff.

We were fed up with doing that. Because it's like . . . We got very, very commercial. All the songs were very "pop". I mean, they weren't sort of very rock. But we just went freaking off in that direction. You do get fed up playing just hard rock all the time. You want to try and do something new, you don't quite know how it's going to turn out. If it turns out shitty, well . . . *Mick Jagger,* 1971.

Whenever I lay the instrumental tracks of a new album for the first time on people I know, you invariably get the same response. . . all the usual bollocks "Oh whaat! It's a new dimension in sound! Nobody'd believe that was the Stones, Blah Blah." I alway say "Wait until you hear Jagger's voice," y'know, 'cos that's a trademark, like an HP sauce label or something. You can't mistake it.

Play the same guys the same songs a few weeks later and they'll tell you "Yeah, it sounds exactly the same as anything else you've ever done." *Keith Richards.*

Were you disconcerted by the general thumbs down 'Satanic Majesties' received?

I can't remember reading the reviews as I was so befuddled at the time.

Actually, I don't take much notice of critics and reviews, but a lot of bands do.

Look, it's only one man's opinion and he's doing it for a living – so in most cases he's a hack. No one can seriously review every album given them with all their heart and soul. It's impossible.

But there are those who take their job seriously.

But a lot of bands, especially new bands, really take reviews to heart and will change their music.

If the reviewers in *NME* and *Rolling Stone* come out and say "This is a load of shit and they should go back to their style of whatever," a band might do it and it might be quite the wrong decision for that band to make. *Mick Jagger,* 1974.

The Singles.

To be honest, I'm not that interested in singles. The band wasn't ever that interested in doing them. It's a very different scene to get into because you get tied to doing follow ups. If you come up with a really good single, it tends to be when you're not thinking about it. There's very few people who can actually sit down and write a single. I've never done that. Nor has Keith. I sat down and wrote one the other night, though, that I thought would be a single. I was quite excited about it. But then I just forgot about it. *Mick Jagger,* 1970.

I miss the old ten inch EP's and I miss singles too, but there's not a singles market anymore. We never sat down to write singles. We wrote songs. When we were in a position where we needed another hit single every three months we could look and say, "That one's the best," and put it out. The fact that you don't have to do it any more means that you don't do it. The art of making a single isn't necessary any more. Which doesn't mean there's a softening in the songs. We still write good songs. *Keith Richards,* 1978.

How did you feel when you went on the Ed Sullivan show and had to change the lyrics from "Let's spend the night together" to "Let's spend

BRIAN JONES, 1967/ERIC HAYES

some time together"?

    I never said "time." I really didn't. I said mumble. "Let's spend some mmmmmm together, let's spend some mmmmmm together." They would have cut it off if I had said "night".
Mick Jagger, 1968.

But they just, by the time somebody gets to a record anyway, have got to realise that even our records have gone through the hands of some of the straightest people you could ever meet. Nearly all the Rolling Stones records – you know this is the first album that hasn't – have gone through this very straight English private fucking company, man. They're the people that are really giving it to you. It's not us that are giving it, we're giving it to them.
Keith Richards, 1971.

We have tried to keep it [the original album cover for Beggars Banquet] within the bounds of good taste. I mean, we haven't shown the whole lavatory. That would have been rude. We've only shown the top half. I don't know when it will be released now. I don't think it's offensive. And I haven't met anyone, apart from two

people at the record company, who finds it offensive. I even suggested that they put it out in a brown paper bag with "Unfit for children" and the title of the album on the outside if they felt that bad about it. *Mick Jagger,* 1968.

Bowie's *Diamond Dogs* cover got banned, didn't it? Well, Ours [*It's Only Rock 'n' Roll*] is really cherubic and naïve by comparison. Not a genital in sight.
Keith Richards.

Decca just never co-operated with us, y'know. They always co-operated with everyone else, y'know. When we were around they just treated us like children. They made a lot of bread out of us. But I'm not in the business just to make money but it does put you a bit uptight. This is like the old fashioned way of dealing with artists. We're just a piece of old thing that you kick around. The only thing they looked after was opera stars, man. And if you don't behave like opera stars you don't get treated like opera stars which is one thing I discovered. Which is terribly draggy to have to perform like that in a fuckin' record company office. But if you just be nice then they just kick you up your proverbial. *Mick Jagger,* 1974.

The money, dear, the money. If you don't go for as much money as you can possibly get, then I reckon you're just fuckin' stoopid! *Mick Jagger,* 1977.

Artistic control? Aw-w come on! We've got that idea sown up, mate. I mean I told 'em [EMI, The Stones European distributor] right there and then, if I go on telly, like, and do worse things and say worse words than what the Sex Pistols *ever* did – will you sack us? 'Cause there's just *no* way you're going to get back any of the money, right? They just said, "No way, Mr. Jagger." *Mick Jagger,* 1977.

You went through a great deal of trouble to set up your own record label and despite this you still encountered heavy resistance when attempting to put the title of 'Starfucker' on the sleeve of 'Goat's Head Soup.' How come?

It was delayed for two months because they're having all this trouble in America with these anti-pornography laws and Atlantic were incredibly up-tight.

That's very strange when you consider that in America you can go into most big record stores and buy a hardcore porn album?

Right. I mean Billy Preston was made to change the title of a song originally called 'All Spaced Out' which was like only an instrumental.

But with 'Goat's Head Soup', they wanted to exclude 'Starfucker' altogether. They got the complete horrors and screamed we're gonna be sued and everyone else got the horrors and I said I don't mind if I'm sued. I mean, I just fought and fought and fought . . . I can't bear it all . . . that finished me.

I said, it's *our* fucking label!

In reality it's not worth it. No, it's not worth the energy I spent on it and the time, trouble and pressures people try and force on me. *Mick Jagger,* 1974.

They've given us a lot of trouble over 'Starfucker' for all the wrong reasons – I mean, they even got down to saying that Steve McQueen would pass an injunction against the song because of the line about him. So we just sent a tape of the song to him and of course he okayed it. It was just a hustle, though. Obstacles put in our way. *Keith Richards.*

Is it true Atlantic Records is trying to get you to delete the song 'Some Girls'. . . or change that line "Black girls just like to get fucked all night"?

Yeah, they tried to get us to drop it, but I refused. Said *no.* I've always been opposed to censorship of any kind, especially by conglomerates. I've always said, if you can't take a joke, it's too fuckin' bad. *Mick Jagger,* 1978.

The Beatles.

In the early days of your career the media seemed to be pre-occupied with a Beatles/Stones rivalry, which became even more acute when the Stones recorded 'I Wanna Be Your Man'. Was this just a press hype or were you aware that maybe the Beatles were immediate competition. and vice-versa?

It's pretty weird when you think about it now – The Beatles were very blasé, – successful, rich. They just didn't seem to care about anything.

Sure they were very creative but somehow they just seemed to regard it all as a joke – and it was. The Beatles were so ridiculously popular, it was so stupid. They never used to play – they just used to go on making so much bread, it was crazy.

Aside from recording a Beatles song, did you get on with them socially?

Yeah, I suppose so, though we didn't really get on with them very much, if you know what I mean. The Beatles were so blasé and, at times, difficult. They would put up barriers which came from I don't know –having far too many people approaching them. They got very big-headed.

It happened very quickly for them in England, they were just young guys from the provinces and didn't want to let anybody know. But at that time, it seemed that every main town in England had some kind of musical rivalry going.

Funnily enough, I noticed the other day when I went to see Mott The Hoople that they still have a different style. Aren't they from the Midlands, 'cause they sound like a Birmingham band to me and they don't 'alf play weird on stage – very different. I can remember the first time the Stones ever went to Liverpool the drummers played completely different. I can't quite remember what it was, but I do know that they played four-to-the-bar on the bass drum as opposed to what drummers in the south played – a more choppy pattern.

They did have a very different sound, and anyway this is all going on, and the other thing was all those harmonies. We didn't have any harmonies, we were much more into the actual playing aspect – quite loose, but nevertheless very tight in our own particular way.

So when we went on the road we vaguely made an attempt to get the harmonies together which was always a bit of a joke. Which they still are. Bad and sloppy. *Mick Jagger.*

Jimi Hendrix.

Jimi Hendrix could play the ass off anyone. I think he was as good a blues player as B.B. King is. I think he could do it standing on his head, you know what I mean? The form of blues, its very . . . his style; like country music. Very stylised. Then you want to break out. Unless you were brought up in that tradition — and none of us were really brought up in any of those traditions — they are forms rather than . . . Well, we *see* them as forms, rather than just plain blues. *Mick Jagger,* 1971.

Oh that's absolute bullshit! Absolute crap, that!! I never *ever* had an argument or a fight with Jimi . . . I mean, we even recorded together, y'know. There are tapes somewhere. Nah – actually Brian once had a fight with Jimi, I seem to recall. Brian loved and idolised Jimi for Christ's sake but . . . that's Brian for you. It was over a chick of course. *Mick Jagger,* 1974

Velvet Underground.

'Ere, but listen, I know who started all that! Lou Reed. Lou Reed started everything about that style of music, the whole sound and the way you play it. I mean, even *we've* been influenced by the Velvet Underground.

Aw, come on, Mick! This is starting to push the bounds of reasonable credibility now.

No, really. I'll tell you *exactly* what we pinched from him too. Y'know 'Stray Cat Blues'? The whole sound and the way it's paced, we pinched from the very first Velvet Underground album. Y'know the sound on 'Heroin'. Honest to God, we did! *Mick Jagger,* 1977.

Elvis Presley.

I never really liked him. Presley hasn't got anyone to tell him what to do and really that's what he needs more than anything else. His trouble is that it was always a question of making money. So Elvis is still fantastically successful . . . Why? Because he makes money and he made his comeback because of Tom Jones or whatever. Anyway that's what I've been told. *Mick Jagger,* 1974.

Is Roy Orbison dead? Hard to tell these days, isn't it? Pop stars — they're dropping like flies. Dropping all over the place, mate. I was in Turkey when Elvis choked it, by the way. They started playing all his records one after the other and eventually I sussed the logical thing — he snuffed it. *Mick Jagger* 1977.

Bob Dylan.

In some ways the impetus of Aftermath *was cut short with the release of the Beatles* Revolver *and Dylan's* Blonde On Blonde. *Was this any cause for concern on your part?*

Never liked *Revolver* very much. I don't like the Beatles.

I'm not saying that I never liked anything they did and I'm not saying that they didn't influence me, because it's impossible not to be influenced by them. I didn't particularly like *Revolver* – I mean, 'Good Day Sunshine', there's nothing in that. It's rubbish, though I suppose there were some good things on the album.

Now *Blonde On Blonde* was a good album. I really liked that.

One could detect certain Dylanesque influences, especially lyrically, in some of the Stones material of that period.

But don't forget everyone was working at the same time, in the same countries, under very much the same conditions – so you're bound to encounter certain similarities. *Mick Jagger.*

Dylan once said "I could have writen 'Satisfaction' but you couldn't have written 'Tambourine Man.' "

He said that to you?

No, to Keith.

What did he mean? He wasn't putting you down was he?

Oh yeah, of course he was. But that

was just funny, it was great. That's what he's like. It's true but I'd like to hear Bob Dylan sing 'I Can't Get No Satisfaction.' *Mick Jagger,* 1968.

It's strange. I spend a lot of my time singing with Mick and Keith and I end up sounding like Dylan. *Ron Wood,* 1979.

Obviously. I mean, it goes without saying. Dylan came along and released everyone from that whole three minute thing, not to mention making it unnecessary to use sentiments based around 'I Want to Hold Your Hand', you know. *Keith Richards.*

Chuck Berry.

My style? Ha . . . I just keep bashing away at it. It's pretty straightforward, but I love to play like that.

I'm still learning, but it takes me an incredibly long while to learn new things. But I'm always conscious of the roots of the music, y'know. I wouldn't like to lose sight of those.

I didn't say I was a rhythm guitarist, other people made my reputation for me. After Brian died I started listening to our records and hearing what people liked in what we'd done. And I realised that what had turned me on in Chuck Berry and people like that, was turning them on in what we were doing. So there's a certain continuity in the whole thing. *Keith Richards,* 1971.

Keith's still playing Chuck Berry stuff . . . [laughs] I try to avoid it as much as possible . . . I mean, I haven't listened to that stuff in years. Rock 'n' roll has always been made by white suburban kids, bourgeois kids. Elton John is a fine example. For God's sake, I listen to the MC5.

Rock 'n' roll's not over. I don't like to see one thing end until I see another beginning. Like when you break up with a woman. D'y'know what I mean? *Mick Jagger,* 1971.

Patti Smith.

I think Patti Smith is crap. I think she's so awful . . . she's full of rubbish, she's full of words and crap. I mean, she's a *poseur* of the worst kind, intellectual bullshit, try-

MICK JAGGER, 1979/MICHAEL PUTLAND/LFI

ing to be a street girl when she doesn't seem to me to be one, I mean, every-thing . . . a useless guitar player, a bad singer, not attractive. I was always very attractive, much better singer, much better with words, and I wasn't an intellectual *poseur.* She's got her heart in the right place but she's such a *poseur. Mick Jagger,* 1977.

The New Generation.

I like to go to clubs that have six bands on in one night, and you see them all and can't remember their names. But I go to concerts and clubs all the time. I don't get so excited about records, I'd rather see the bands live. A lot of the new bands don't record well anyway. *Mick Jagger,* 1977.

Whatever is new needs a few years to

COVER OF 'EXILE ON MAIN STREET 1972

develop in some little corner somewhere where nobody knows about it except a few fanatics. Like The Beatles did, like we did, like Presley and Chuck Berry and Fats Domino before him. *Keith Richards.*

Punk!

First off, that bit about Johnny Rotten slamming the door in me face outside of Malcolm McLaren's "Sex" shop is a lot of rubbish. 'E only says all those *nasty* bits about me, 'cause 'e loves me so much . . . Now this is all total fantasy. Just complete and utter fantasy. I never read it – but oh dear – no, it's not true at all. I don't even know where the "Sex" shop is . . . hold on, I vaguely recall where 'Let It

Rock' used to be. But there's a lot of clothes shops in the Kings Road, dear, and I've seen 'em all come and go. Nobody ever slams the door on me in the Kings Road. They all know I'm the only one who's got any money to spend on their crappy clothes . . . though even I would draw the line on spending money on torn T-shirts! *Mick Jagger,* 1977.

Many of the English punk records sound like our early records, and that sound is very hard to achieve nowadays. But it seems to be the sound many of them are aiming for.

We did them on a two-track Revox

in a room insulated with egg cartons at Regent Sound. Under those primitive conditions it was easy to make that kind of sound, but hard to make a much better one. Today the new bands are having to work against environment, sophisticated technology, 24 track studios.

So, what happens is that you end up with someone like Glen Matlock — who in terms of songs has been one of the biggest forces behind the English punk movement – bringing Ian McLagen into the Rich Kids' lineup. So straight away there's a direct connection with the Small Faces.

Like I said, there's no way you're going to break those connections . . . that line. Sure, you do get concerted efforts like the Sex Pistols, but that was studied. It was as much Malcolm McLaren as Andrew Oldham was our early high powered publicist. *Keith Richards,* 1978.

Punk, punk, *punk*. We're a punk band, one of the few.
You're punks and you're staying at the Fairmont with police escorts for your limo? C'mon Mick.
Shut up, shut *up*. It's the *attitude* that counts! *Mick Jagger,* 1978.

Reggae.

I'm drawn to reggae because there's nothing happening in Black American music. They're going through the disco phase. It's very popular and no wonder people are drawn to it. The temptation to make those records is strong.

Reggae took off because there are more Jamaicans in Britain and America than there are in Jamaica! Bob Marley has created an international status for reggae and now Africa will be a big market for the music too.

Trouble is, I don't know if Roots Reggae is what people want to hear from me. I've been playing mostly reggae with Tosh's band and either I cut some more to make a complete album or I'll leave it in the warehouse. When I've got an album's worth of material in front of me, then I'll think about releasing it. I've got Robbie Shakespeare on bass, Sly Dunbar on drums and Robert Lynn on piano.

As far as I'm concerned, I'm not white and they're not black. It's just something you don't think about. They make me feel very comfortable when I'm working with them. I've been going to Jamaica for over ten years. People will say "Oh he's doing his reggae bit." So I might just put my reggae recordings into the vaults until it is more acceptable to people.
Keith Richards, 1979.

'Ere, 'ows the Prisoner From Ile De Re, then? *Mick Jagger,* 1974.

The Shams.

Bands have always been into copying us. Really, I mean, what were bands like the Pretty Things and Them with Van Morrison doing back then?

Nah, it's not a piss-off and it's not particularly flattering either. I always wonder if they're just doing it for the bread or basic considerations like that.
Keith Richards, 1975.

What do you think about bands, like the New York Dolls, who deliberately try to copy the Stones?

Well I only know that they sound like the Stones 'cos people tell me that they do. I've never actually seen them working. I've seen the photos and it's obvious that the

guy [David Johansen] mimics Mick, and he does look incredibly like him.

I mean if you think about it you have to conclude that it'd be better if they had their own thing entirely. I'm sure they'd be happier if they were making it on the strength of something a little less tenuous than having a guy in the band who happens to look like somebody that's rather more famous.

No one has yet succeeded in sounding quite like the Stones?

Not consistently, but then I think that's a dumb idea anyway. The whole problem with them trying to sound like us is that we've had twelve years experience. Not that experience counts for a lot in rock. God you look at a lot of these old rock 'n' rollers, experience counts as a hindrance more than a help. Look at Chuck Berry now. I laugh down my fucking sleeve that the guy ever turned me on.

How can somebody that epitomised the whole fucking thing by consistently making great rock 'n' roll records, sound like that?

Everybody's looking for something new but there isn't gonna be anything *new* cause they're sapping up every bit of talent the minute it rears its ugly head. No one has time to develop, they've got to make it right away. Suddenly you're a Mainman artist or a Rak artist. Now they're forcing Mick Ronson on people. They're lucky they got away with Bowie let alone Mick Ronson. Ya see, the thing is they believe their own fucking mystique. They don't realise it's all bullshit, all propaganda.

But if you're asking does it bother me . . . no, it doesn't. *Keith Richards.*

Oh Gawd, Aerosmith! they're just rubbish – absolute bullshit. The singer (Steve Tyler) is a quite a nice guy, mind you. He's almost too bloody sweet. He's very kind to me, anyway [smirk]. Yeah, you know what I mean. He's such a little sweetheart, really – what can you do with him? Punch 'im in the mouth? 'Ere, what are you playin' at, fuckin' impersonatin' me? – Slam! [laughs]

Ugh, the New York Dolls. What a load of rubbish! Iggy's all right. I saw 'im with David Bowie on that last tour – the band was pretty ropey I thought.
Mick Jagger.

The Nature Of Our Game.

What's your exact name? We might as well get that straight.

Yeah, that Richards/Richard thing, people think it has some mystical relationship to the band or that particular record. Y'know the old bone-earring trip. It's thanks to Andrew Oldham that. He was a great one for names. He had a few odd ones for himself. Sandy Beach, I think was one. Anyway, it was Andrew who decided to knock the 's' off me name for some reason. So for years and years I remained in the singular, everything was printed with no 's' until [grins] I started to wield some influence over the printer and sometimes it gets on there.
Keith Richards, 1977.

School Daze.

I'd like to do something completely different. There's too much pressure being in a group: if I don't wanna do something, they do, and vice versa. I'd like to take a year off and study.

Study?

Yeah.

Back to LSE?

Nahh. I've got a few projects . . . [He looked reticent] I think it's all just talk.
Mick Jagger.

What kind of education do you envisage for your daughter Jade?

A very varied one. I'd like her to go to an ordinary school so that she'd understand all sides of life. I don't particularly like education over here.

Well, the whole system appears to be on the verge of breaking down.

[Laughs] I don't know – I haven't been to school lately. It *was* when I was there and it doesn't seem that much different now.

I mean, there were forty in a class at grammar school and how the hell can you teach forty grammar school kids at a time? It's impossible. It's much better to have six in a class like when I went to college at sixteen, and that's why I got a reasonable education.

As a matter of fact, I took a correspondence course in History and French. *Mick Jagger.*

I've seen it from both ends. I've seen it as a kid after the war, and in the sixties, for instance, in the early Beatles and Stones days. That was probably the most affluent period that England had, the late fifties and early sixties.

But now it's happening here, too, they're just churning them out of school and there's nothing for them to do. That would have happened to me, except they said, "Oh look, he's good at drawing. Send him to art school." That's where probably half of England's rock and rollers have come from, art school. You wouldn't believe how many of them.
Keith Richards, 1976.

I wouldn't want to put my own or anyone else's children through the sort of education that's available nowadays, especially in England. In England it's to do with making your station. The school system is turned into a model for life, with prefects as policemen and Headmasters as Judges.

It's all about preserving the order of things which has always existed, and very little to do with learning. Learning is something you have to receive from wise men and there are very few of them around.

There are new methods of learning now, they've got to be exploited in the future. There are a lot of subjects that don't require teachers – who may be good, bad or indifferent – subjects where you're better off with earphones and a talking tape, and the chance to think for yourself, instead of having to cope with the hang-ups and inadequacies of some

CHARLIE WATTS, 1965/GERED MANKOWITZ

schoolteacher who hasn't even sorted his own problems out.

People at the moment are just made to learn in order to get qualifications in order to get money in order to get more money, and there's not even a hint that there's something beyond that.

At school, for example, I had a good time in economic history – I loved it – but they always said: "If you want to learn X you have to learn Y". I was made to do double entry book-keeping if I wanted to study economic history. I hated book-keeping. You can do that with a calculator, and they know that, but they still keep you at it to teach you your place.

Here in America it's already changing, the student movement has brought that about. Here you could do a thesis on the Rolling Stones if you wanted to. Mind you, I'm not saying that's better than studying Plato.

You have to be careful about what is pumped into children before the age of seven. That old thing of St Ignatius, you know . . . ? *Mick Jagger.*

When you think that kids, all they really want to do is learn, watch how it's done and try and figure out why and leave it at that. You're going to school to do something you wanna do and they manage to turn the whole thing around and make you hate 'em. They really manage to do it. I don't know anyone at that school who liked it or anyone my age who liked to be at school. One or two people who went to a decent school had a good teacher, someone who really knew how to teach. The nearest thing I been to it is Wormwood Scrubbs [an English prison] and that's the nick. Really, it's the same feeling. *Keith Richards, 1971.*

Love & Marriage.

Did you really phone Paul McCartney the night before his wedding and tell him not to do it?
I would never tell anyone not to marry someone. I approve of them . . . a beautiful couple . . . a lovely couple . . . all the same I wouldn't let my old lady play the piano.
Mick Jagger.

Marriage? It's all right for those who wash.
Mick Jagger, 1967.

Getting married's really nice, as long as you don't get divorced afterwards. It's very important that you shouldn't get married if you think that you could get divorced.

Divorce is just that legal part of it, you know, the legal way out of it. I think if you want to get married and you consecrate your union to God, you can't break it, not even with God. You just have to carry on. I think marriage is really groovy. *Mick Jagger, 1969.*

What can I say but rumour brings mischief. She's quite . . . uh, pretty. I can't imagine bein' married now either. I tell ya, I mean my old lady, I don't know what she'd say. She'd probably scream at me in Spanish or something. But I wouldn't recommend it. I don't think personally it's necessary. I feel the same about it. I carry on the same and I find it works. You might find that contradictory but everyone's life's contradictory innit?
Mick Jagger, 1970.

When Mick first saw me . . . he had the impression he was looking at himself. I know people theorize that Mick thought it would be amusing to marry his twin. But actually he wanted to achieve the ultimate by making love to himself.
Bianca Jagger, 1974.

I've done everything I could to hold our marriage together, but in the end it was impossible. It's been a heartache. I thought Ann might be persuaded to return, but now I know she would not. We may have thousands of fans around our feet, but you're a pretty lonely man if you haven't got a family to go home to. If I hadn't been a Stone, perhaps it would have been different. But my career was in the way, and I know in my heart that this was to blame. The Stones' success took us all over the world — and away from home. We coped pretty well until two years ago, when we found ourselves struggling to make the marriage work. Then Ann went off to Durban, South Africa, to live with relatives.
Bill Wyman, 1975.

I love it when people tell me I'm so settled down and domesticated. For me it's one hotel to the next. I rented a house in New York for a while, which was nice. I'd never done that before. I've always lived in hotels.

I do try to hang out with different

MR. AND MRS. JAGGER, 1972/KEYSTONE PRESS

kinds of people but I'm usually around music business people. You find yourself going to studios on a busman's holiday singing backup vocals. I was going back to college for a while, but I never made it. I'm a real dropout. I wanted to do comparative religion and history, but I just couldn't take three months off and go every day. I found myself having to work, and I'm just too lazy. I need three months off from music, but I can never get them. *Mick Jagger, 1977.*

Be that as it may, you've always appeared to have maintained a regular lady. How important is a prolonged relationship with a woman to you?

Actually, if you're a musician I think it's very good not to be with anybody, and just live on your own. Domesticity is death.

You see, the trouble with most musicians is that they're too domesticated. A musician doesn't spend too much time at home; he's on the road living out of a suitcase. Then when he gets back home he tends to become very domesticated.

In fact, you enjoy the best of both worlds. It's taken me years to start buying furniture – I still don't have hardly anything and what I've got is falling to pieces.

I can't stand to stay in one place for too long. I'm not trying to say that women aren't important – they are. I like my lady to come with me, but I don't like to stay in one place in the same way as say The Faces or David Bowie who spend an awful long time at home with their old ladies and families. *Mick Jagger.*

[While the Rolling Stones were being photographed with Margaret Trudeau] I wouldn't want my wife associating with us. *Charlie Watts, 1977.*

Children.

Having kids has changed me, I'm a lot more relaxed. Previously, I always acted like I was on the road even when I wasn't Y'know I lived in hotels and looned all the time. Now I can come home, which is great.

But . . . [with a shake of his head, the world's most famous earring swinging into view], I don't like habits. I couldn't stand to be with the kids all the time. I need to be able to take off for a couple of months now and again. *Keith Richards.*

If two people love each other they shouldn't be worried about a piece of paper. We're talking about marriage on pieces of paper, where if the husband leaves the wife or *vice versa,* the children will be guaranteed to have some money. But they should be able to arrange that, if they're reasonable human beings, they

LONDON 1967/SYNDICATION INTERNATIONAL

should be able to at least look after their children without lawyers in wigs having to do it. That's ridiculous. *Mick Jagger, 1969.*

My parents, or my generation's parents, think that their offspring are very strange. But I can already see, from my friends that have already had children, that these children are going to be so strange and so far apart from their parents, so different, completely — they're going to be almost twenty-first century children. And that's going to be very difficult for the parents. *Mick Jagger, 1969.*

Aren't you concerned about protecting young Jade [Mick's daughter] *from the traumas that have beset the Rolling Stones?*
    [With a fine scorn] Traumas? I haven't had any. I haven't had to go to Vietnam and get napalmed, or jump out of helicopters and shoot peasants.
    I mean, getting nicked is nothing. It's just like getting a parking ticket. All you have to do is to make sure that whatever you do doesn't bother other people. That's something worth telling a kid. You can even talk about discipline if you're careful. Everyone has to have a code. Everyone has to be tied down to something, but within discipline there's a lot of room to move and that's not often mentioned.
    On tour we have a lot of discipline:

people to move, equipment, deadlines, union things. I can talk about all that kind of discipline to a child because I can understand it and I can cope with it. Maybe I'm a frustrated Army officer. *Mick Jagger, 1973.*

As a parent, all you can teach a child is what you've learned yourself. I could give a child a reasonably good sex education and I think I should as a duty.
    Babies and adolescents are preoccupied with sensuality. If you withdraw children from sensuality it affects them in later life. [Grins]
    I didn't invent that. It was R. D. Laing I think. The most you can teach kids etc. etc.
    It's wrong though, to be over-protective. Everyone benefits from what God puts in front of them. If you set your sights low, if you duck out of too much danger, you have a very boring life. *Mick Jagger.*

The Media.

The summer is the worst time because they have so little to write about. It used to be the silly season. Now it's called the sick season. I think they really must have run out of news. They think you're fair game, but it's a bit annoying.

Thank God I don't live here all the time now. If I did it would be a nightmare. England, Germany and Italy are the worst countries for gossip. Here they just write pages. But there's nothing new about it. It used to be movie stars. They dished the dirt on everyone in Hollywood.

Have you ever read *Hollywood Babylon*? They dished everyone and a lot of those scandals were made up. And it affected their careers in those days a lot more than it does now. Big movie companies would drop people if they got into trouble. They would protect them to a certain point and then if there was real trouble they'd drop them and their career would be finished.

I know in certain instances record companies aren't keen to take on a band because of their image, like EMI and the Sex Pistols. Because the group behaved in a certain way, the company just kicked them out. *Mick Jagger,* 1977.

It's all so far removed from reality. All that stuff you read in the papers about me and Bianca, it's like a page out of someone else's life. It has no relation to me at all. It's completely made up.
Mick Jagger, 1977.

It doesn't put me off in the least. On the contrary, I like talking to people. I think everybody needs the media to a certain extent but I tend to think it manipulates you as well because as soon as you become popular, you are in a sense public property and have to find yourself featured in stories that are invented purely by the press. Some of them are true and some aren't. I don't think there's any harm in that as long as you don't identify too strongly with your public image. I think if you do that you run the risk of losing your own identity.
Mick Taylor.

Well, there was this local guy from the *Merseybeat.* I don't know who he was, can't remember his name, but he was diabolical. Actually I've still got the press cutting at home because they did a whole centre spread in the paper.

The interview was held in the dressing room and we took the piss out of the poor guy from the start of the interview to the very end. We didn't let up for

a moment. Everyone told him totally wrong facts and made outrageous quotes and he wrote the whole thing down dead seriously. While he wrote he kept on repeating, "It's true what you're telling me? I mean, you're not putting me on, are you?" And we'd reply straight faced, "No, we wouldn't dream of it."

Before the guy came into the dressing room Keith and I had noticed these two slightly curved metal discs about the size of half crowns lying on a bench. But we couldn't figure out what they were used for. Anyway, during the interview I casually picked one of these discs up and put it in my eye like a monocle . . . you know, just messing around. Well, this guy noticed me doing this and enquired what did I use them for. Without thinking, I told him, "I have to wear these on stage because I have something wrong with my eyes. I suffer from conjunctivitis and I mustn't be exposed to bright lights. I can't wear dark glasses because they show up, so when we go on stage or appear on television I stick these discs over my eyes to protect them. Naturally I can't see anything, but if I do want to see, I just look out of the corner of my eye."

Well, we carried on talking about this, and the rest of the band were creased up with laughter behind him. Would you believe that he swallowed the whole thing and in the next edition of *Merseybeat* there was this whole story that I had told him, complete with a big photograph of me with one of these silver discs over one of my eyes. It was so stupid, but you had to laugh. *Bill Wyman.*

'Ere, I'm not going to tell you what Bob Dylan and I worked out that we were going to do to Scaduto but . . . [he chuckles to himself].

'Ere, but Mick, I thought Bob Dylan was Scaduto's mate.

Not any more, I mean the deal was for that Dylan book. Scaduto forced him . . . well, it's none of my business to say any more about Bob but I'll tell you what he did to me. He sent me a letter, right—I've still got it as a matter of fact— where he stated words to the effect that he would write a really nasty book about me unless 'quote – unquote' I co-operated with him. I mean, what do you do in those situations? I just wrote back and said 'Go ahead and write what you want' and we'll see what happens [cryptic smirk].

Another thing – Greenfield's book S.T.P. I recently discovered how he wrote that. I recall him being on only four or five of the dates we played in the States, right, and for those he came along simply as a writer from *Rolling Stone*. What actually happened was that he got to see a lot of the rushes from Robert Frank's film 'Cocksucker Blues' and wrote it from there, which is ridiculous because there he is writing with supposedly great authority about almost every juncture of the whole tour and he's getting most of it from film footage, again from which, at the best of times, you can't get anything approaching a decent perspective. *Mick Jagger, 1974.*

You see, I don't really give a damn what they — what the media or whatever you call them — write about me. I'd just like to see all those cock suckers spending an hour on stage doing what I do, and see how they stand up to it. I just presume they have nothing better to do, or that they're hard up for a story, or whatever.

It still goes on and I just go along with the "Bad publicity is better than no publicity" idea. I mean, if they wrote about me as the sweet, gentle, loving family man, it would probably do me more damage. And be equally untrue. *Mick Jagger.*

High Fashion.

The image that came across in the fan magazines at that time seemed to portray you as extremely narcissistic?

Of course we were, every fucking band is narcissistic – that's the whole fucking trip. They all think they're beautiful, even the ones with the bent noses and the goggly eyes. We didn't think we were pretty like some bands, but we thought we were bloody good.

Now I consciously dress up. Some people go on in what they arrived in, and there's no harm in that, but I find blue jeans don't pick up the light too well from the back of an 18,000 seater. *Mick Jagger.*

But I must say I do not share the foppish notion that clothes make the man . . . in fact, I am more inclined towards the opinion of the late great Al Einstein on the subject . . . one time when his wife begged

him to "go out and get yourself a decent suit of clothes for God's sake" he replied "it is of no consequence, after all, one does not judge a pork chop by its wrapper". But still, all in all, a bit o' swank never hurt a flashy act, don't you agree? *Mick Jagger, 1975.*

I don't think Mick needs to be so conscious of what the rest of the rock hierarchy are doing, you know. He always wants to know what everyone else is doing and sometimes I get the feeling that he measures himself on what he does against that which he shouldn't bother with. He shouldn't take any points from himself as to what Bowie's doing or Zeppelin. When he's been away from playing Mick gets into the business end and tends to see it too much like product. *Keith Richards, 1976.*

I'm afraid most rock and roll stars are just interested in themselves. You go on a stage . . . you get egotistical, of course you do. You think you're really important, and you're not. I don't think anyone in rock and roll is important. We're all full of shit. As a performer you do need an ego but that doesn't mean it's any good. *Mick Jagger, 1977.*

I remember the time I was turned away from a club in Sidcup because they thought my trousers were too tight. What sauce! But I got out of it all right. I put on the tight ones and then another pair over them, and when I got inside the club I just slipped the top pair off. Very shrewd, eh?

I was just thinking, it's amazing how people change their tastes in gear. Take, for example, the fact that not long ago all of us Stones were in boots. We were crazy about them. Now I wear just plain, black lace-ups and Mick goes in for two-tone suede and leather casuals. Keith is the only one who still sticks to his Chelsea boots. *Bill Wyman, 1964.*

I have two suits and five jackets. Don't buy much. I'd rather save the money. *Keith Richards, 1964.*

It appears quite extraordinary that a man of Mr. Keith Richards' stature could only have one pair of trousers. [Judge at Aylesbury End Court in response to Keith Richards' excuse for a two hour delay due to a laundry error, 1976]

I see leather's back in this year . . . Very tasty! *Bill Wyman,* 1974.

I enjoy changing personalities.
Really?
Yeah, honestly I feel I've got to be very uh . . . chameleon-like just to preserve my own identity. You have to do it sometimes . . .
But doesn't it reach a point where you lose contact with yourself?
Hmm, maybe that's true, but I don't feel threatened by that possible eventuality. I don't want to have just one front. I feel like I need at least two just to carry on doing what I'm doing comfortably. It's acting, sure it is . . . that's what it obviously comes down to. It just gives me the facility to do practically anything I want, see, and even then the most drastic changes of personality don't really affect me 'cos I never feel the need to do 'em that often. It's all part of being a rock 'n' roll star, after all.
Mick Jagger, 1977.

I'd hate to be Mick. I'm glad to say he's promoted himself in that direction –always in the magazines– because it helps us. It's great for me because I'd never do that. I hate that sort of thing. I'd hate to go on stage and walk around in front of everyone. *Charlie Watts,* 1978.

I hate sloppiness of any kind!
Brian Jones, 1966.

I cut off great handfuls [of curls] and give them to my fans. *Bill Wyman.*

Crew cuts were never popular in England and putting grease in your hair. And we can't be bothered to dress alike. We had jackets alike once. It was a big drag carrying them around. *Mick Jagger,* 1966.

Some Friends & Acquaintances.

I certainly don't want to go on stage and just stand there like Scott Walker and be ever so pretentious. I can't hardly sing, you know what I mean? I'm no Tom Jones and I couldn't give a fuck. The whole thing is a performance of a very basic nature, it's exciting and that's what it should be. The idea of doing it all over again is a drag. I'd like very much to have

someone produce a show with us. I'd like that, I'd really like to do that.
Mick Jagger, 1965.

Mick had always dug visual artists himself. He always loved Diddley and Chuck Berry and Little Richard for the thing they laid on people on stage. He really dug James Brown the first time he saw him. All that organisation . . . ten dollar fine for the drummer if he missed the off beat. *Keith Richards.*

When we go on tour, we'll be putting on a show, because people will expect it of us, and I couldn't just stand there and sing. It applies to everybody, even the Pink Floyd do it. There are very few bands that don't put on some kind of a show, except somebody like Paul Simon. His show is raising an eyebrow, or hearing a pin drop. But that's still a show. I think our tour will be a bit of a laugh. We're going to have Billy Preston playing piano and three brass players, and the stage setting will look nice. *Mick Jagger.*

We want to put on a good show, visually, as well a givin' 'em an earful. But in England it's just *all ears.* Has to be. 'Ow can you put on a spectacle in a bloody garage. I mean most stages 'ere look like a bicycle shop with guitar leads everywhere – really messy. The trouble with England is everything is so scaled down compared with America. There's not enough space for us to really prance about. It's no good complainin' about it. It's the way it is. "It was good enough for Shakespeare, me boy", that sort of thing. It's kept 'em going for five hundred years, so why bother.
Mick Jagger, 1970.

Erotic tussles on stage with Bill and Keith? It wouldn't work. I tried. They wouldn't take any notice. They wouldn't take any notice if I took their truss off.
Mick Jagger, 1973.

I find the society thing, that scene, very easy. I've been involved with it since I started, ten years ago, although I've had my times of reaction to it. There were times when I thought it was nice to dress up in sort of flashy clothes and be fashionable, which I did in fact for years in London. After coming from a drab background, it was chic. *Mick Jagger.*

MICK JAGGER WITH LULU, LOU REED, DAVID BOWIE AND FRIENDS/PICTORIAL PRESS

Andy Warhol? We work well together. We've talked about doing a film of Gide's *Caves du Vatican,* stage designs, a musical, a set of lithographs of me. I dunno. When girls get together, there's always talk but they never get anything done. *Mick Jagger,* 1973.

Gotten Rich Quick.

Getting rich quick is all part of the rock and roll fantasy. For most people, the fantasy is driving around in a big car, having all the chicks you want and being able to pay for it all. It always has been and it still is. Anyone who says it isn't is talking bullshit. I'll tell you, I could never have gotten as rich as I am through any other means.

Sure, there was a period around 1968 when people did object to rich rock stars — like, being rich wasn't considered to be cool. But I wasn't rich then. I remember doing a tour of Europe around that time and there were these people turning up at our shows and handing out these revolutionary leaflets which said that we were ripping the kids off. Well, all I know is that at the end of that tour we all came out with £1,000 each — and, in fact, I came out with much less.

A lot of people have got this attitude that they've just got to get rich quick, because if they can fill Madison Square Garden now they better get as much money for the tickets as they can because they might not be able to do it in a year's time. Which, for a lot of bands, is the truth. I do concerts for everything, every time . . . the joy of performing, the birds and the money. Now, if I only did it for the money I wouldn't be playing with the Rolling Stones, I could go and do, say, Wembley on my own, charge 25 p a seat and still make money. But if I wanted to get as rich as I possibly could then I'd play Las Vegas as a solo wish.

If you take a million dollars and divide it by eight, it doesn't amount to much. It might be a lot to you, and maybe I'm just jaded. To me, a hundred thousand dollars doesn't buy very much. You can live on it all right for a year, but you can't buy a house and a car with it. People think I came away with a million dollars, and unfortunately that's not true. I worked very, very hard on that tour. But I'd make much more money from a movie than doing that.

Living up to an image is the biggest drag about touring. The only way I can do it is to be their idea of Mick Jagger all the

time. It's not a strain once I get into it, but it can make you irritable. Because of the pressures you tend to be rude to people and be obnoxious and conceited. It's important to keep this to a minimum. But I don't think people mind if I'm conceited.

I don't set out to be like Cassius Clay or Alice Cooper. I don't say that I'm the best in the world. I let other people say that if they wish.

Every rock and roll star in the world is conceited. *Mick Jagger,* 1975.

Would you do it all over again?

No. Of course not, after you've done it once *[laughs]* Surely that's more than enough.

I'd like to do something else but we're taught from a very early age that failure is the worst thing that can happen to a person. For instance, in school the one who can give the quickest answer is the teacher's pet. They'll pick on a kid that's a bit slow and demand. Why don't you know the answer? The whole class knows and one kid doesn't. Jesus, he's made to feel inferior.

It's not a team it's more like a trial by ordeal. So whether we're gonna be soldiers or rock 'n' roll singers we've got to be the best – we mustn't fail and everyone has gotta be fuckin' trampled under foot, and you *do* have to trample other people under foot.

Why? Because someone has got to win and someone has got to lose – and that's not what music's about at all. It's not on.

The industry and society, the media and everything else foster competition in every field. Especially in pop music or in any field of entertainment. You're just built up to be put down. A footballer is built up to be put down and it's the same with a musician – manipulated by the media and by the people who control them.

How have you managed to retain your equilibrium?

You've either got it or you haven't.

I mean, life is scarey, and everyone's got to go off the deep-end sometime or other. You can't remain perfectly stable all of the time.

Just being on stage or recording is a great outlet for one's neuroses. You can get rid of all your fears or pent up energies sing songs or just screaming and carrying on while you're up there on stage. Some people are neurotic and some people aren't and some people can see through things, while the others get taken in by them – taken in by all these games.

I mean, why do people want to be popular? People vying in competition – in the charts which is like a rat-race with the claws fully bared. The competition for adulation, admiration – physical and intellectual. It's a very bizarre way of carrying on.

It's all right when you're seventeen. You don't know these things, you just do them. You want to be popular with all the girls on the beach, but after a while you start to think: Why do all these people do it?

Money! Money is pretty level-headed compared to all the other things you want. If you want money at least there are things you can do with it. But it's adulation that most people are after.

When you attained success, were you elated or disenchanted?

I was elated, but struck through with cynicism, 'cause you can't help laughing at the funny way people behave. Whereas before you were plain ordinary, now you weren't – you were suddenly being treated in another way. The thing is, you just don't know how people are going to treat you until you've reached that level that you thought you wanted to reach.

When you reach it you may not like it, which accounts for the way a lot of people behave. They work hard for success and when they finally achieve it they don't like it or can't handle it – there's hundreds of those. I don't mean obvious Casualties Of Rock, as some of you call them in the music papers. Just people that you know who can't handle their success or fell to pieces when they lost it. *Mick Jagger,* 1974.

I'm a family man, I suppose. I keep myself to myself. Mick and Keith are the only two members of the group who go around with each other. I'm about the only Stone who has the same relationship with friends I had before the group started. *Bill Wyman,* 1966.

Do you know who your friends are?

Yes, of course – but I like to make new friends. I'm not one of those people who just sticks with the people I knew ten years ago.

There must be people who want to befriend you for who you are, as opposed to what kind of bloke you are.

Yeah, but I think I can sort those ones out pretty quickly. I know the people who like me. *Mick Jagger, 1974.*

I don't have people hanging around. It upsets me to see Rolling Stones casualties but it's not the Rolling Stones that destroy people, it's themselves. They shouldn't hang out. I don't have anyone hanging out in *my* room. Nobody except the band. What are *you* doing here? *Mick Jagger 1976.*

I Believe.

Mick do you believe in the Lord?

Sure, I believe in the Lord. All my life. And I believe in gospel music, I believe the Lord's in gospel music. I learned to preach from Little Richard. I don't preach as much as I used to. I just play guitar now, that's all I want to do. Woody and Keith helped me learn. Brian would never help me out. The only numbers I preach on now are 'Eyes' and 'Beast Of Burden' Keith wrote that. Most of it. I wrote most of 'Before They Make Me Run', but it was Keith's idea. *Mick Jagger, 1978.*

It's kind of limiting using your intellect to write songs like 'Brown Sugar' innit? The only thing I'm really interested in is Comparative Religion and Ancient History. *Mick Jagger,* 1976.

My values change all the time. Everybody's do. The things we thought were important last year don't seem to be quite so relevant. Maybe it's not so much changes as getting away from things that aren't very important. Like one year you think to be on your own in a huge hotel room is really beautiful and the next year you may be thinking about having a family and living in a room in San Francisco is where it's at. Yeah, it changes. *Mick Jagger.*

It's a drag. But you have to take the rough with the smooth and be grateful for small mercies and other such homilies. I'm happy . . . I'm as happy as one can expect to be with the knowledge one has. You can't expect to be divinely happy until you divinely work on it". *Mick Jagger.*

Miraculously, due to abstinence and prayer my teeth grew back!
Keith Richards, 1979.

STATE BALLROOM, KILBURN 1964/BRIAN ARIS